CASTING AT THE SUN

CASTING AT THE SUN
The Reflections of a Carp Fisher

CHRISTOPHER YATES

PELHAM BOOKS
LONDON

PELHAM BOOKS

Published by the Penguin Group, 27 Wrights Lane, London
W8 5TZ, England
Viking Penguin, a division of Penguin Books USA Inc.,
375 Hudson Street, New York, NY 10014, USA
Penguin Books Australia Ltd, Ringwood, Victoria, Australia
Penguin Books Canada Ltd, 2801 John Street, Markham, Ontario,
Canada, L3R 1B4
Penguin Books (NZ) Ltd, 182-190 Wairau Road, Auckland 10,
New Zealand

Penguin Books Ltd, Registered Offices: Harmondsworth,
Middlesex, England

First published 1986
First published in paperback by Pelham Books 1991

Copyright © Christopher Yates 1986, 1991

All rights reserved. Without limiting the rights under copyright
reserved above, no part of this publication may be reproduced,
stored in or introduced into a retrieval system, or transmitted, in
any form or by any means (electronic, mechanical, photocopying,
recording or otherwise), without the prior written permission of
both the copyright owner and the above publisher of this book.

Filmset and printed by BAS Printers Ltd
Over Wallop, Hampshire

ISBN 0 7207 2004 4

A CIP catalogue record for this book is available from the British
Library

To the memory of
RICHARD STUART WALKER
an angler more complete than Walton
AND
JACK (THE ROADMAN) FARMER
one of the last, true countrymen

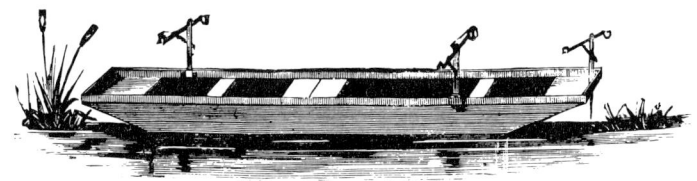

THE GODS DO NOT TAKE FROM A LIFE
THE TIME ONE SPENDS IN FISHING.

Abyssinian inscription 3000 BC

CONTENTS

Foreword by 'B.B.'   9
Preface   10
Acknowledgements   11

PART I – IN EARLY DAYS
  1 Another World   14
  2 Remembering Mr Green   18
  3 Treasure Island   22
  4 River Interludes   29
  5 The Tea Gardens   34

PART II – THE WAY TO THE WATER
  6 A Roving Rod   46
  7 The Overgrown Path   52
  8 The Haunted Pool   62
  9 Thunder and Potatoes   70
 10 Pilgrimage to Redmire   80
 11 A Night Foretold   85
 12 The Bell at Byton   88
 13 Oakwater Epitaph   94

PART III – REDMIRE
 14 A Village Cricket Mentality   102
 15 Variable Weather   113
 16 A Pot of Gold   120
 17 Redmire Reflections   127
 18 Autumn and a Carp to Remember   135
 19 A Classic Opening   145

PART IV – CARPS AND BEER
 20 The First Four Days   163
 21 Far From the Madding Crowd   171
 22 The Winchester Request   178
 23 Golden Hours   183
 24 Parker's Bag   193

Contents

PART V – REDMIRE REVISITED
  25 The Monsters of the Myth   205
  26 The Mystery of the Redmire Teapot   214
  27 A Record Carp Story   216

PART VI – THE LAST CAST
  28 Earthing the Current   226

FOREWORD
BY 'B.B.'

Little more than half a century ago nobody appeared to take any interest in carp or carp fishing. Then appeared a delightful book, *Coarse Fishing*, by H. T. Sheringham, editor of *The Field*. Included in it was an account of how he caught a sixteen-pound carp from Cheshunt reservoir and when I read this it triggered something off. I republished Sheringham's piece, together with the few other carp stories I could find, in my own *Fisherman's Bedside Book*. That great angler, the late Richard Walker, read my book one Christmas and such was his interest that he soon got in touch with me with the idea of forming a carp catchers' club. By pooling our experiences of this mysterious fish we discovered more about it, and now there are carp fishing clubs all over the place and some monstrous fish have been brought to bank. The largest so far was caught by Christopher Yates, the author of this excellent book, which has given me hours of great enjoyment.

The reader will find his opening chapters especially nostalgic as he describes so well the intense excitement of the small boy who first begins to fish, and how even the most ordinary village pond seems to hold mystery.

I have corresponded with the author of this book over a number of years. He is something more than a fisherman. He has a deep interest in nature. I have letters from him from time to time from his remote cottage in a Surrey vale, about the purple emperors round his door, badgers near, and birds innumerable.

Your good fisherman must also be a good naturalist: the author is such a man. I recommend this book unreservedly to all fishermen who can find the quiet hour by pond or stream full of interest, peace and a deep enjoyment.

'B.B.'
August 1985

PREFACE

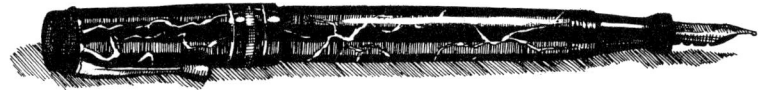

This book was written with a fifty-year-old fountain pen. It is about days spent beside old ponds and lakes, often in the company of old friends, fishing with old tackle for old and sometimes very big carp. And though most of the stories are also old, only a few of them have been published before. The events I describe range from the comic to the tragic, the strange to the dramatic; but they are all true – even the daft tale of Walton's rainbow is true.

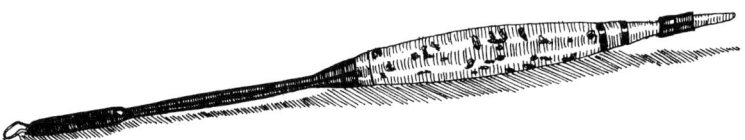

VALE COTTAGE
September 1985

ACKNOWLEDGEMENTS

This book would never have been finished were it not for the encouragement of others, who should really have known better.

Firstly, I'd like to thank Sandy Leventon, who, as editor of *Angling*, was not only the first person in history to get me to work on a regular basis (I wrote a monthly article), he also persuaded me to continue working on the book that I'd stopped writing five years before. The late Richard Walker also encouraged me into the writer's chair and I shall always be grateful to him for his professional advice.

To 'B.B.' I give special thanks for honouring me with the foreword to this book.

My two typists, Karen Steedman and Anne Scott, deserve endurance awards for managing to wade through the original manuscript, somehow making sense of all my crossings out and scribbled corrections.

Nigel 'Parker' Haywood read the first half of the book and gave me the kick up the pants I needed to finish the second half. He also went through the manuscript with an examiner's eye, occasionally ending up on the floor laughing at a nonsensical phrase. I thank him for his correcting pencil and for chivvying me to the final full stop.

And, of course, I must thank Gaffer, also known as Clare, my marvellous wife for illustrating my stories so beautifully. As well as being a very fine illustrator, Gaffer also cooks the greatest eel pie in the universe, and her smile is as warm when I leave to go fishing as it is when I come home again.

PICTURE CREDITS

All the photographs in this book were taken by the author.

The engravings are from the author's collection of historic fishing books, and the pen and ink originals, which were specially commissioned for the book, are by Clare Hatcher.

PART I

In Early Days

Minnows were not despised, gudgeon were greeted with rapture, and the occasional triumph of a roach, with gorgeous red eyes, was a thing beyond words.

H. T. SHERINGHAM *An Open Creel* (1911)

I
ANOTHER WORLD

WATER – the fresh water of pure rivers and lakes, is alive, vibrant and serene. It is also colourful, moody and, especially when deep, mysterious. There was even something mysterious about the village-pond near my childhood home. Not only was it a better place for toy boats than the bath, its green depths held unseen monsters.

At first, I only knew of these monsters through the stories told by the fishermen. I used to watch these anglers with a keen interest and though I never saw any of them catch anything, I recognised, even as a five-year-old, that they fished not so much with patience, but with a quiet, contained excitement. I was told that their colourful floats were the links between them and certain fantastic-sounding creatures that lived in the deepest places in the pond. Though I did not see any of those painted corks and quills actually move, there was something dramatic about the way they cocked upright on the still surface, like guards standing to attention. And there were great tales about those times (how long ago? I wondered but never asked) when a float did disappear and some colossal fish ploughed away towards the sunken willows.

Because I didn't see anyone catch or even get hold of a fish, I wasn't sure whether to believe these fishing stories. For all I knew they might prove to be as sadly fictitious as all those stories in the children's books I'd been brought up on. It was encouraging to see grown men looking so eager and behaving so enthusiastically, but I realised that it might prove to be a rather involved and complex game of make-believe, like playing conkers with an imaginary opponent.

I was, as I said, five years old when I first began watching the fishermen, and I was a rather sceptical child. But too many illusions had been shattered; ever since I discovered the lie about Santa Claus, half the world had proved to be a sham. However, I had to confess there was a change in the way I looked at the muddy pool. Especially in the evening, when all the picnickers and barking dogs had gone home, I seemed to sense a shadowy transformation. Perhaps it was just my imagination, but then perhaps the pond really did harbour monsters. In the twilight, with the darkening of the glassy-still water, it seemed quite possible.

Then, one magical day, when I was walking round the pond with

my father, I saw them. It was a bright, late-spring morning and, out by the small island in the pond's centre, the water suddenly erupted. A shoal of huge, golden-scaled fish began charging through the surface, leaping and somersaulting. As we watched, they surged off in a glittering phalanx towards the willows on the east bank. With a few last tumbles and plunges, they disappeared under the hanging greenery, leaving great waves and ripples spreading across the entire pond. (They were spawning though, obviously, I did not realise this at the time. Only when spawning, do fish mass together like that and completely abandon themselves to their annual frenzy.)

I would have been satisfied to have seen just one of those great fish, but there must have been about thirty. I was dumbfounded: happily amazed to discover the truth of the legends, happily surprised to discover how impressive the truth looked. It was like stumbling on a pit of dragons.

Later in that year, when my father and I were again walking round

the pond, we came upon an old angler in the willow-shaded corner. He looked the picture of contentment, sitting on his wicker creel, leaning forward, elbows on knees, gazing through a haze of pipe-smoke towards his distant float. There was a large keep-net lying in the margins and we could see something inside. We asked the old man what it was and, in answer, he reached forward, took hold of the end of the net and gently lifted it up. Lying in the mesh was one of those same gold-flanked fish we'd seen in the spring. It stirred, wallowing half out of the water. Close to, it looked enormous. Beautiful and also terrible. The most miraculous thing I'd ever seen.

"What is it?" I asked in a whisper.

"Carp," he said, lowering the net back into the pond.

Creatures from another world, then, didn't just reputedly haunt the water, like a tale in any boy's book of adventure, they *actually* haunted it and, what is more, it was possible to connect with them.

Was it strange that my infant imagination should have been stirred like this? There was no logical reason for it. Only the fishermen, who were strangers, had told me anything about the pond, and being naturally quiet-seeking they really only hinted at things and didn't give much away.

I had no friends or relations who fished. As a child, the very existence of carp would never have become known to me had I not lived close to the pond. Yet those fish affected me like sparks on petrol.

2

REMEMBERING MR GREEN

THE old village of Burgh Heath, Surrey, had a friendly, comfortable atmosphere – a genuine village with none of the cold, raw tidiness of the 'Best Kept Village' competitions. It was a cluttered, shambling hotch-potch of old cottages – each with a little garden crammed with flowers – and small shops, pubs, church, school and stables. On the west side there were the Tea Gardens and the pond – Burgh Heath pond, with its tiny, but distinctive island and the broad, sweeping willows.

I would like to say that my house was in the old village, but it wasn't. I lived in a dull 1930s house, amongst other dull 1930s houses that were huddled between farmland and heathland to the east of the village, across the Brighton Road (when I lived there, that road was narrow and quiet; today it is like a motorway). From school to home was about four hundred yards, yet I usually managed to double this distance, especially after I'd seen the carp. I would run round the back of the school, race past the terrifying geese that grazed an acre of grass, cross a road, pass through the middle of the village and so come to the pond. For five or ten minutes, I would gaze intently at nothing at all, then go home for tea. I never saw anything. But my mind boggled with the thought of all those mysterious fish. Where did they hide? Could they see me? Were they oblivious of everything that happened on dry land? What did they do with their watery days? I never saw them, but they would come home with me and swim through my dreams.

Watching the water was sufficiently exciting in itself for a year or two. Though it was inevitable that I would eventually fish, I knew as a small child that I was too timid and insignificant to challenge even the smallest carp. And, when I was about eight, I discovered that while the bent-pin-and-string-on-a-stick was fine for the writers of boy's stories, these fanciful people could never have tried this absurd method themselves. It was enough to drive a lad to tiddly-winks.

In 1955 my family moved to a larger house a mile distant from the pond and, because I didn't see the water as regularly, the dream of the golden fish became less vivid. But on my eleventh birthday, I had a postal order for seven shillings and sixpence and nothing particular to spend it on. Browsing through my favourite toy-shop I discovered a boy's fishing outfit — a three-piece bamboo rod and a packet of assorted tackle, the whole mounted on a display card. It was the illustrations on this card that sparked the old fire. Three drawings depicted first a boy fishing by a river, then the boy's rod bent double and finally the boy hauling a monstrous fish *through the air* towards him.

The 'outfit' cost me five shillings and as I opened the shop door to go out I didn't realise that I'd finally opened that door in my head, a door that would lead me to countless different waters, always in search of the same elusive dream, a door that opened wider and wider as time passed and which has now fallen off its hinges.

I went back to the pond, approaching it now with a wondrously heroic spirit — a proud knight on his first quest. With my 'proper' tackle, I was capable of anything and I cast a worm with a clumsy but confident sweep of the rod. After five minutes, I began to grow impatient. I cast again and again. I tried a number of places where I had seen the other anglers fish. My float bobbed stupidly in the ripples and I called out to the carp, accusing them of cowardice. I felt hope evaporate. I went home. I returned, determined to sit it out all day. But, after an hour, I left the rod to fish for itself and went over the heath to hunt for lizards (at least I knew I could catch lizards).

After another frustrating day, the pond sparkling so promisingly in the early-morning sun, and shadowing so blackly in the evening, I lost all hope. It seemed the task of even getting a fish to bite was completely beyond me. To catch fish you needed not only special knowledge but special powers. I had neither. I would never be able to match the heroic deeds of the old man by the willow, or the young angler pictured on the boy's fishing outfit.

Then, I remembered Mr Green.

Mr Green was our next-door neighbour. A year previously, my father had dug a fish-pond in our garden. Just after it was finished, Mr Green appeared on our doorstep with a bucket containing eight dark-looking little fish. "I got these gudgeon from the river today," he said. "Would you like them for your pond?"

Mr Green, then, was an outstandingly successful angler, for though gudgeon were not as awe-inspiring as carp, he had caught *eight*. However, since that day I'd not had an opportunity of talking with him again and,

In Early Days

until I was driven half-mad by the irresponsive fish, I wasn't bold enough to knock on his door and ask him to share his secret of success with me.

He was my last hope and as soon as I blurted out my first question to him (before I actually spoke, I'm sure Mr Green suspected, from my sullen expression, that I'd come round to confess some evil sin – like raiding his strawberries), he smiled cheerily and said he'd be delighted to help. I showed him my fishing tackle, and he wasn't very impressed, in fact he seemed to mutter something disrespectful about the makers of such 'toys'. The rod, he said, was too stiff, the float too big and the hooks simply incredible (I remember that they were the most curious hooks; shaped like a capital 'G'). The line, said Mr Green, was only good for flying kites. Only the reel had his approval, and that hadn't come with the 'outfit'. My father had bought it for me from a genuine tackle-shop.

All this was tremendously encouraging. I knew it was a bad workman who blames his tools, but this was different. A good workman had told me so.

I was advised to get hold of a smaller float, a packet of *real* hooks (size 12) and a spool of five-pound *nylon* line. Lastly, I was persuaded to be, initially, less ambitious. Carp were exceedingly cunning and powerful fish, so it would be sensible to leave them out of my plans for a year or two and concentrate on smaller, less demanding quarry.

Money-boxes were dredged, transactions for advance pocket-money completed and my large-hearted father cycled down to Epsom to buy the essential items. And on the day before I made my ultimate challenge to the lesser monsters of the deep, Mr Green called to me from across the garden fence and said he'd got something for me. He passed over one of his fishing rods. It was a present to me.

Since that day, I have many times been impressed by the kindly acts of generous anglers, but that gift of a *real* rod, to a boy who had never even caught a fish before, is the most charitable thing I can remember. And it wasn't just the rod – a beautiful, light split-cane eight-footer – it was the confidence he showed in me by offering it. He knew I'd waded too far into that private pond in my head and that I could not just give up and stagger back into the dry world. But I needed help, so he gave me the rod and the faith to bend it.

Such was my ensuing optimism, I even took a jam-jar when I set off the next morning. It was grey, breezy and warm when I arrived at Burgh Heath Pond. I carefully tackled up, baited with a small worm and cast about twenty feet out. The rod felt alive after the bamboo poker I was used to. My slim, red-tipped float rode nicely on the incoming ripples. After a few minutes, with no warning at all, it just ducked under. (Since that day I've seen thousands of other suddenly sinking floats, yet that first astonishing disappearance remains the most memorable of them all.) I upped with the rod-point and felt a spine-burning tug on the line. It was true. It was not a dream. I did appear to be reeling something in that glittered silvery on the grey water. Indeed, I was soon holding a real live fish in my hands. It was about four inches long and had silver scales flecked with purply-blue. As the universe looked over my shoulder it was obvious that I had caught a gudgeon. Just like Mr Green.

I reverently placed the fish in the jar of water, packed up my tackle and loaded it onto my bicycle. Then, holding the jar aloft with a trembling hand, I rode triumphantly home.

3

TREASURE ISLAND

Burgh Heath Pond was an ideal water for a young angler. In the summer of 1959, when I first began fishing, I spent almost all of my school holidays sitting by that acre of greenish water. No days, not even the slow drowsy days of July, were long enough for me. Had I been allowed, I would have set up camp on the bank and lived the life of an enthusiastic heron until the school inspectors took me away in September.

All the important things in boyhood were beyond the sphere of ordinary, everyday life; yet it often happened that the cold voice of logic would undermine the pleasures of, say, marbles, or cowboys and indians, or conkers, or the conquest of the world. I'd realise that these things were not really sound enough to endure, that they would become boring, like train spotting or stamp collecting. Fishing, however, was not like any of these things. It was strange and it was also real. At times, it could be a very serious business, something you had to devote all your mind to. It was always entertaining and exciting; full of wonderful contrasts – disastrous and triumphant, tragic and comic, dramatic and tranquil. It had mystery, corresponding to certain vague, indefinable dreams. But, best of all, it was your own secret joy and no one else could govern or share it.

As the summer progressed, so did my ability. I caught more gudgeon and I also discovered perch. Perch are splendid, striking-looking fish with yellow scales, bold black stripes and bristling red fins. The pond's perch were sometimes voraciously hungry. I remember one that was so hungry that after I'd caught, admired and returned him, he immediately grabbed my worm again when I accidentally cast short into the margins. I had to carry him round the pond and let him go by the marshy reed-bed where no one ever fished.

All the perch I caught were small – up to eight inches long – but one day a veteran fisher of perch came along and caught a monster so staggeringly huge that it troubled my dreams for a week.

At first, I fished alone, but then my brother Nick came to see what all my fuss was about and he immediately saw the point. He went off and got hold of a crazy, yard-long metal rod, complete with a moulded-on plastic reel. With this contraption he caught a perch *first cast*. It seemed almost unfair, after all my early trials. But Nick slipped easily, almost casually, into the business of catching fish, while I had probably been too earnest and serious. It was my first lesson in the psychological approach to angling, made all the more startling every time Nick caught a fish on his bizarre tackle.

Parental law allowed us to fish until sunset, when the pond always looked at its most promising. The surface stilled and the bats came out to skim across it, mingling with the evening swallows. At that time, with

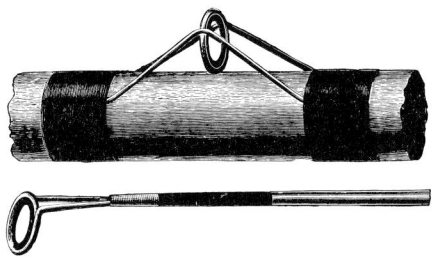

the shadows beginning to thicken, I would imagine the carp emerging from beneath the willows. It was always a wrench to pack up and cycle home.

Two similarly afflicted school boys, David Austin and Derek Dawson, joined us for our second summer on the pond and it was with them that we made our daring crossing, by bicycle, to the island. This island, with its distinctive weeping ash tree, had always looked remote and inaccessible. We had never seen anyone else conquer it and we had never tried to wade across ourselves as the water was too deep for our gum-boots (we had learned the painful way that it was perilous to wade bare-footed – the pond-bed was strewn with reefs of broken glass). One day, someone suggested that if we *pedalled* to the island we would be high enough in the water, as long as we kept to a shallow causeway, to reach it safe and dry.

Being the most reckless, David went first. After carefully securing all his gear, he swooped down the bank and disappeared in a cloud of spray. Away he sailed, his half-submerged front wheel forming a bow wave, his rear wheel churning up a fountain of muddy water. Pedalling madly, his boots sloshed the surface like a scrambling duck. Five yards short of his goal, he teetered dangerously, but with a final effort lunged forward and was soon waving triumphantly from the island. I went next, followed by Nick and, apart from a few worrying moments when the wheels sank and slipped in the silt, we both made it safely across.

Derek was not so lucky. Half way through his voyage his hull struck something substantial. In slow motion he keeled over and his ship went majestically down with all hands. The captain went in up to his knees. Since he was wet, he thought he might as well grope around underwater for the offending article and, after a moment, he heaved up a weed-festooned milk-crate. It was curious that we others had missed it completely. He hurled it into deeper water and, pushing his bike, began to wade towards us. He looked a real ship-wrecked mariner and we couldn't help laughing at him.

When you are young and daft and have just conquered the only island in the village pond, you see yourself as a bit of a Captain Cook or a

Long John Silver. We were the first boys to have voyaged across the western straits on bicycles: all we needed to do now was find the buried treasure.

The island resembled the archetypal desert island that cartoonists like to portray. It was small, just a rough grassy tussock about a yard high and twelve feet across. Instead of the usual palm tree, we had that single, outspreading ash and we each sat with our backs against its trunk, fishing the four corners of our domain with an enthusiasm only a boy could understand.

We were casting into virgin water for, though we knew almost every inch of the bankside, the area round the island had always been out of casting range. Straightaway, we began to get bites, those bold, float-stealing bites that we knew from experience meant that the perch were on the feed. Derek caught the first one and immediately his dampened spirits lifted. Even his socks began to dry.

We all jumped up as soon as the colourful, stripe-backed pirate landed on the grass. The first fish of the day always had a strong magic about it (it still has), but on that day, on the island, the perch seemed especially dazzling.

"A half-pounder!" we shouted, even though it wasn't even a quarter-pounder. We popped it in the keep-net and returned to our fishing, each

of us silent and intent until, a few minutes later, there was another bite and another cry of "Got one!" Then three rods were dropped and the lucky fisherman had all the attention.

The sun climbed higher and a few other young fishermen began to appear on the bank. We felt pretty smug as they looked across at us.

"Landlubbers!" yelled David, and we all chuckled. Then another bite distracted us and soon a third bristling perch was having himself intensely admired.

We were using brandlings for bait and on that June day the perch went mad on them. After an hour, we had caught almost a dozen. And as well as perch there were also numerous gudgeon and, to our great amazement, someone (I don't recall who) caught a rudd. It was the first rudd we had ever seen. The floats were never still for more than a minute and there was hardly time to open a bottle of Tizer.

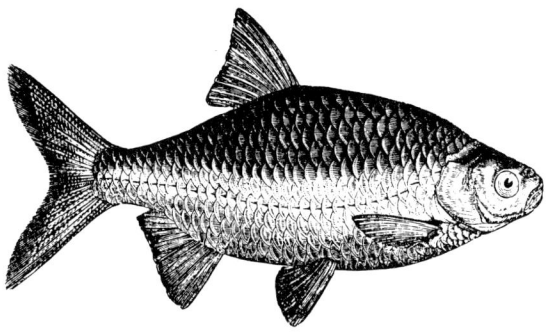

On the mainland, things were not happening at all and the natives were not amused by our continual yelps of delight. At midday there was some ominous displaying of catapults and the natives seemed more interested in collecting pebbles than fishing. We began to get anxious, not because we were afraid of flying stones, but because we knew the fishing would suffer if there was an elasticated bombardment. After our success we guessed that many other anglers would follow in our bike-tracks and, in future days, the island's fishing would never be as good again. It was our red-letter day and we didn't want it spoilt. So we reeled in and quietly set about our sandwiches and pop, praying that a few minutes' inactivity would cool the natives' wrath. Naturally, as we ate our picnic, we surreptitiously prised pebbles out of the clay bank and placed our own catapults at the ready – just in case. (In 1960 no one had ever heard of a 'baiting catapult' and ours were used strictly for offensive purposes.)

Our withdrawal policy seemed to be working, but what would happen when we began fishing again? The problem was solved by a man angling in the hallowed Tea Gardens, behind the willows on the pond's north side. Someone spotted him hook a big fish which turned out to be a tench. Nobody in our world had ever seen a tench before and everyone on the bank jumped up and ran off towards the willows, leaving their rods and catapults behind. Even we islanders debated whether or not to cycle ashore and witness the earth-shattering miracle. Like the carp, a tench was a mythical creature and it seemed important to behold the real thing.

However, the way things were going, it was quite likely that we might catch a tench ourselves, so we decided to stay put.

In ones and twos the mainlanders returned from the Tea Gardens. They shouted across that the tench was 'the biggest thing you ever saw!' Perch were ten-a-penny according to one boy who had actually touched the monster. We were quite pleased with all this; the capture of the tench had completely eclipsed our own achievements and, what is more, *we* were now the underdogs, the unfortunates who had missed the miracle. The atmosphere calmed, catapults were put away, everyone began peaceably fishing again and we continued to fill our keep-net.

Though the sun blazed down, the perch never lost their appetite for worms. We caught little ones and ones not so little, though the biggest was not over six ounces. (Big perch existed only in dreams and fishing books.) But, though we caught no monsters, we were so delighted with our netful of plunder that, every so often, we'd burst into spontaneous laughter. Each of us seemed to be catching the same amount of fish so there was no unhealthy sense of competition.

The sun began to sink towards tea-time and we remembered the promises we'd made to our mothers. Would they believe us if we said the tide had risen and cut us off? The pop bottles lay empty in the grass and there was nothing left to eat, yet our hunger for the fishing was still keen and we would have happily forgone teas for the rest of the week if only we could have fished for one more hour.

We knew we were going to be late home, but no-one could bear to call for the last cast. Slowly, we began clearing up and putting away our bits and pieces. Eventually, there was nothing left to pack up but our rods. We reeled in and tied all the gear to our bikes. Then we ceremoniously hauled in the keep-net, enjoying a few moments' high fever as we gazed down at the striped flanks and crimson fins. We had a long, last look at the splendidly coloured rudd — the real treasure of the island — then we let them all free. A burst of small bow waves exploded away from us.

After such a day we could have cycled across the North Sea. The voyage back to the shore seemed so effortless we wondered what all the fuss was about earlier — it was no more difficult than pedalling through long grass. Quietly, we cycled round the pond. The banks were deserted, but as we came opposite the Tea Gardens we could see the old tench-fisher still crouched by his rod. We looked back to the island, then again at the gardens. There was no denying it; though the island was definitely the best free area on the pond, the Tea Gardens had an even more exciting and tantalising appearance. It was a secluded, willow-hung area, with a shady lawn bordering a really delectable piece of water. There were even seats. But it cost half-a-crown to fish there and that sort of outlay (almost a week's pocket-money) was unthinkable when the rest of the pond was free.

Through the curtain of willow leaves we could see the evening sunlight glowing on the red roof of a cottage. On the tiles, painted in large white letters, were those evocative words, 'Tea Gardens'. It was probably the most splendid place on earth for, besides tench, it was there, according to legend, that men battled with carp. *Carp*!

4

RIVER INTERLUDES

SEVEN miles from home was a winding, lively little river. Now and then, our mother would treat us to a day out and a change of venue, driving us down to the water in the family car – a pre-war Morris Eight. The river was the Mole, where it runs between Mickelham and Leatherhead.

For the first few visits we caught nothing but minnows. But we could crawl under the willows and look down into the shaded water. A single ray of sunlight would flash on the flank of an otherwise invisible fish, or a dark shape would materialise from the depths, revealing itself as a chub, which tilted upwards to take an insect from the surface. Once we saw a gigantic pike, lying crossways in a shallow slack, his fins working gently and his prehistoric head pointing towards a shoal of seemingly carefree dace (we'd learnt to identify the different species of fish from our growing library of angling books).

It was the vivid transparency of the water that I liked most about the river. You could stare in and actually see fish. The pond, on the other hand, had the clarity of strong, milky tea – it was like a window with a curtain across it. The river had no curtain and its marvellous interior was visible to anyone who cared to look. You could lie along a willow bough, or hang over a high bank, and survey a different world. The contours of the river-bed were pockmarked and cratered, like the surface of the moon; the swaying weed streamers were like trees in a steady gale; the fish were like fantastic birds, soaring through the varying currents on thin, almost invisible wings.

Fishing in such a magical setting, it didn't matter that we caught only

minnows. And besides, there were real fishermen (as opposed to fisherboys) who could show us the grander inhabitants of the river; big roach from a certain, almost inaccessible eddy – beautiful fish with flanks like blued steel and fins like rose petals; bronze bream from the deep, dark channels; great blunt-headed chub, far larger than any we saw under the willows – these fish were usually taken from beneath rafts of flotsam, or along streamy runs where hanging bramble bushes combed the surface.

One August day Nick and I decided to explore further downstream from the familiar, minnow-infested pools. We followed the bankside path until we came to where the river flowed through a dense and tangled wood. I guessed that, where the water darkened, extraordinary fish would be waiting to pounce on our baits.

However, it was not easy to penetrate the wood. The path ended abruptly at a high, ivy-grown fence and, mainly because of our rods and tackle, it was difficult to crawl through the only narrow gap in the wire. Once under the trees we were immediately aware of an eerie stillness. Just upstream, the river tumbled and chuckled as it ran over gravel shallows, and the fields on either side were wide and bright. But the water was deep as it wound through the wood and the current slowed to silence. The banks were steep and so thickly overgrown with yew and box trees that even we, master tunnellers of hedgerow and thicket, could not snake our way through to the water's edge. We pushed further into the wood and eventually found a place where the trees thinned and allowed us a clear view of the river. It looked black and bottomless and was undoubtedly haunted by monsters. A foot above water level was a chalky ledge, just big enough to accommodate two smallish anglers. We clambered down and prepared our rods.

Full of expectancy, we cast, watching our floats as they drifted lazily downstream. They turned, eventually, to be whirled slowly round a deep eddy. Within minutes, my yellow-tipped quill curtseyed and slid sideways – not at all like a bobbing minnow bite. I braced myself, struck, and up came a perch no bigger than anything from the pond. But it was more brilliantly coloured and strikingly marked than any fish we'd seen before. In the dark of the wood, it looked unreal. A few minutes later, Nick landed one – the same size, the same brilliance. We caught half a dozen and every one was as bright as coloured glass.

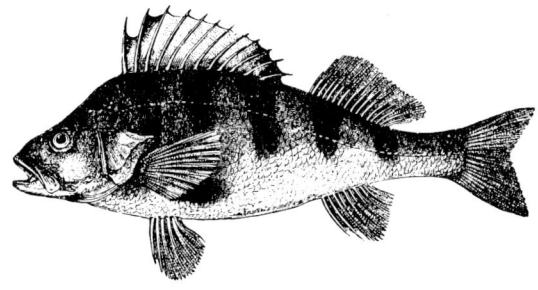

The expedition had been a success, but just as we were thinking of packing up, there was a slow, heavy splash under the opposite bank. What was it? Crocodile? Hippo? The dark reflections coiled and wobbled, then the surface calmed and we kept our eyes fixed on the place where it had broken. The water was shallower on the far side; we could just make out the pale river bed and, dark against it, a fish showed clearly. It was a huge chub. He was obviously just waiting for morsels of food – fat caterpillars and drowned flies – to come drifting down to him. He looked as if he would snatch the first worm cast near him. But even if we did succeed with the long, tricky throw under the branches, such a fish would be impossible to land. We had no net and, anyway, our tackle was too feeble to cope with monsters. It didn't matter; the glimpse of that chub would fuel our imaginations for weeks and give a new importance to our fishing talk. Catching sight of a big fish can be as exciting as catching the fish itself.

For various reasons, I didn't return to that stretch of river until the next summer. When I did so, I went alone, on my bicycle. It was a still, sultry July day and the fields by the water shimmered in the heat. The image of that great chub was getting clearer in my head the nearer I drew to the wood. For no good reason, I felt sure something momentous was going to happen.

I reached the wood, but didn't enter it. There was a shingle bar that jutted out into some shallows just where the first trees leaned over the river. By standing on this bar, I could cast a float to the opposite bank and let the current take it down the leafy aisle, into the monster's lair. By a fluke, I dropped the float, first cast, into exactly the right track. It swayed and dipped as it passed by the current-deflecting roots, but it kept its course. I had to crouch down and narrow my eyes to keep it in sight. It blurred amongst shadows and reflections. Then it was gone.

Had it pulled under or was it simply lost from sight? I hesitated, then tightened the line, and the rod-top was dragged over. It bent into that same sort of arc as those straining rods depicted in fishing books. My boots scrabbled on the loose stones as I steadied myself and tried not to be tipped into the river. I hadn't learnt that an angler gives line to a powerful fish, and that was why I was fighting with my feet to stay on dry land. I presumed, if all else failed, that the line or rod would break, but whatever happened, that fish was not going to be given an inch.

After a while, the strain eased and I began to feel less precarious. I wound in a few yards and saw the line cutting up from the surface, slanting directly towards the alder roots. Yet nothing jarred; the thing I was attached to allowed itself to be drawn past a dozen treacherous snags. Perhaps it just wanted to have a peek at the impudent boy who'd had the gall to stick a splinter of steel into it: just a glimpse, before smashing me.

Suddenly, I saw it. Out of the olive shadows rose a grey shaft with a black tail. It cruised serenely past me and carried on upstream, the rod bending round after it. Its swimming became laboured and though the tail kept fanning, the fish slowed to a hovering stop. Before I could believe it was happening, it reversed into the gravel bar and, without much assistance from me, grounded itself. Whether it was the monster we'd seen before is unlikely, but it was certainly the biggest chub I'd ever seen on the end of a line. It turned on its side and wallowed, yet it didn't look exhausted; it just looked bored. A more obliging fish would be difficult to imagine. Feverishly, I bent down and scooped it up onto the shingle. It hardly flapped a fin. Perhaps it was simply too overwhelmed to respond, but whatever the reason I was extremely grateful. I'd caught a big chub. A terrific chub. Its scales were larger than my thumb-nails, its head was

as big as my fist, its tail as wide as my hand. I, naturally, had no spring-balance: such a gadget was an unimagined and unnecessary luxury; but I did possess a 'fisherman's ruler'. The fish was nineteen inches from nose to tail. Truly a Leviathan, I thought. Yet, though I was jubilant I felt I couldn't compare him to a carp. He was big, brassy and splendid; but lacking the carp's majesty, he could not be awarded full honours.

I carried him down to the water's edge, let his image sink deep into my mind, then slipped him back. Immediately, he snapped out of his quiet dream. He kicked with his tail and streaked away, blurring quickly into dark water.

5

THE TEA GARDENS

AFTER the sparkling river, Burgh Heath Pond could often seem shrunken and dull. In hot, dry weather, when the marshy reed beds became more exposed, it sometimes smelt like a compost heap. The water was always thick and soupy but compared to the clear depths of the Mole, it looked like glue. Never, though, did it appear tame. In fact, the murkiness made the pond more fascinating for it obscured the great fish you knew were there. There were places on the river where you could fish and see virtually everything that was happening, but when you cast into the pond it was like reaching into a treasure chest with a bag over your head.

For three seasons I fished enthusiastically for anything that swam. Simply being conscious of the carp's presence was enough; a direct challenge was unnecessary. I sometimes arrived at the pond with the grand idea of spending the whole day in pursuit of carp, but I lacked the confidence or patience to sit it out. My plans would soon be modified to allow the use of a small hook, tiny redworms and light float tackle, which ensured that I happily caught nothing but perch or gudgeon.

There were, however, several instances when it seemed the carp had lost *their* patience with me. Once, fishing next to the willows, I hooked something that just swung sideways, taking me with it. My float cut neatly across the surface, then a fish crashed magnificently into the submerged branches. The float arrowed back again, flying through the air. The line had snapped just below it.

What should I have done? What *could* I have done? I looked despairingly across the water, like an admiral who'd just seen his flagship go down.

One rainy afternoon, fishing on the other side of the willows, I watched my float sink down so slowly that I wondered whether it had become waterlogged. I gave a casual, half-hearted strike and there was a mighty eruption of spray and the sudden, glorious sight of a big, gold-plated flank. For a few moments I felt the electrifying, piling pressure – and then it was gone and I was left staring at the outspreading ripples.

The greatest disaster of all happened not to me but to Nick. He hooked a carp well away from the willows, over by the island. Three of us had been fishing the same bit of water – Nick, Mike and myself – and we all shouted in surprise when Nick's little rod suddenly curved almost flat. There were no snags, apart from an old car tyre, and Nick just hung on tight as the fish ploughed first one way, then the other. His yard-long rod bucked and quivered, but abiding by the Boy's Rule of Battle, he never gave an inch of line. (I've never understood how his tackle stood the strain.) Eventually, a fabulous creature surfaced next to his wellingtons. After a moment's hesitation I waded forward and pounced on it, grasping it across the back with both hands, feeling a sudden shock at that first contact. It shook free and bolted forward towards Mike. He shuffled round until he'd got the carp between himself and the bank, then he tried to flip the fish up onto dry land with his *boot*. As he kicked, so did the fish and Mike's foot neatly severed the line.

If we had left the whole business to Nick, I am convinced he would have 'won the day'. As it was, Mike called me a blithering butterfingers and I called him the new village idiot. Nick said nothing, nor did he ever quite forgive us.

Throughout those times we were constantly aware of that other more tantalising world that lay out of our reach in the midst of the willows. Often we would stand on the one short stretch of bank that gave you a clear view of the place – the angler's Utopia, the castle of our sky – the Tea Gardens.

Now and then you could see men sitting like statues by the water and if you called across to ask them if they'd caught a carp they were usually too engrossed or too irritated to reply. But now and then you would get an answer like news from the field of Saint George. And something sensational was always happening. A big carp had battled for half an hour, finally diving under the willow and almost pulling the angler in. Or a carp was triumphantly landed, only to break the spring balance when it was weighed. We still dreamt of fishing there, but the dream was getting old and we were growing impatient.

The stuff of our dreams.

Once we climbed out into the willows that grew like a mangrove swamp round both sides of the gardens, and swung from bough to bough across the water until we came in sight of the small, clear bay where the anglers fished. Then a voice like a rusty razor cried out: "Clear off, you boys!" It was the terrible Tea-Lady, an ancient battle-axe with a reputation for tyranny and ferociousness. Where the Tea Gardens were concerned, she had absolute authority. We always imagined her as some kind of malevolent she-spider. Now there she was, a barrel-like shape just beyond the last curtain of willow leaves. We were out of range of her stick, but only just. We fled like squirrels. And we only wanted a closer look at the place! Gawks! What would she do if we actually walked right up to her and asked permission to fish? Her awesome presence gave the Tea Gardens an even more exquisite aura.

My first carp was caught, appropriately enough, from the place where that old angler had shown me his catch, many years before – the 'quiet corner' on the opposite side of the willows from the village. It was Midsummer Day, 1962. The weather was breezy and warm, with frequent soft showers interspersed with flashes of bright sunshine and I arrived at the pond determined not to be diverted by tiddlers. I had the same curious self-assurance that I'd felt once or twice before; a quiet inner certainty, completely at odds with my usual lackadaisical nature.

Wading out a few yards, I cast into a small bay formed by a break in the willow boughs. My bait was a large piece of fresh bread-flake squeezed onto a size 6 hook; my float was a big yellow-tipped porcupine-quill carrying four B.B. shot. It was not long – perhaps only fifteen minutes – before the quill slid decisively across the surface. It slanted into shadow, under the trailing leaves and I knew, absolutely, that this was *it*.

The sun was shining at that moment, right in my face, so I didn't exactly see what happened when I struck. There was a splash and the rod heaved into a half-circle. I think my eyes must have begun to water for my vision suddenly blurred completely and all I could do was pull to the right, away from the forest of snags. Then my sight returned and I saw a wave break on the edge of the greenery. There it was, churning the surface. The pressure was telling, the carp was coming out into the clear, sending the spray flying. I moved steadily away from the willows, leading the carp into open water, and after a bow-waving tussle I began to draw him towards me. I still had no landing-net, but I was lucky. Behind me, the water shallowed gradually to a smooth clay bank and so I was able to beach my fish easily. He lay on his side, flapping weakly, and I fell on him with due reverence.

The golden scales seemed to blaze when I laid the fish in the wet bankside grass. A real, palpable, wonderful carp. A nine-year-old dream fulfilled. How big? It probably weighed a little over two pounds.

Mixed with the jubilation were a few moments' hilarity. A stern woman suddenly appeared and rebuked me for bringing a live fish to the pond just so that I could pretend I'd caught it there! Was she being serious? She was. I laughed and tried to explain, but she did not believe me. "There are no fish as big as that in this pond," she asserted. "What is it, a cod or a salmon?" She called me a few unkind names and stomped off, leaving me stupefied – but only for a moment. No madwoman could break the spell of that morning. I put the carp in a keep-net and, for the price of an ice-cream, sent a runner to tell my family the news. Then I re-cast and, before long, I'd hooked and landed a second carp, a fish of about half the size of the first. An hour later, even as I saw my mother and father cycling round the pond (Nick was playing football and missed everything), I landed another. (They were all true wild carp.) Three carp in a morning! I felt as if I was a bell that had been struck heavily three times.

Before that Midsummer Day I had been quietly haunted by the image of a gold-scaled fish in green water, but afterwards I became obsessed. The only cure for my fever lay within the Tea Gardens. It had been forbidden to me for too long, first because I could not afford it and then because I was too afraid to face the old witch. But now my pocket-money had increased and my fever had made me reckless. "Tomorrow," I told Nick, "I'm going to fish in the Tea Gardens."

"Good-oh. I'll come too." His tone made it seem no more important or perilous than tree-climbing or kite-flying.

The great day dawned and, as I'd prayed, the sky was blue and the sun rose clear and bright. I wanted it to be hot, knowing that a blazing sun would keep the carp in the willows' shade. We tied our gear onto our bikes, pedalled away along the road and then up the steep narrow path, between gardens, onto Burgh Heath. As we rode along, I thought back to all the anglers I'd ever seen at the Tea Gardens. There had never been any youngsters and we had often been told that no boy would ever be allowed to fish there. But there was always a chance that the Tea-Lady might relax the rules, at least for a day. And, whatever else, she wouldn't eat us – would she?

We bought some chocolate from the sweet-shop that overlooked the pond then, leaving our bikes leaning against a fence, we gathered up our tackle and walked, rather hesitantly, along a narrow, overgrown path. The path led round the side of the sweet-shop to the Tea-Lady's cottage. I knocked politely on the door, but no one answered. I held my breath and knocked again, less politely. After a moment, we heard a scratching and shuffling from within. It sounded exactly like a big spider scuttling over a bare floor. The door opened and we stepped back. Leaning on her stick, the great Tea-Lady came hobbling out into the sunshine. Close to, she appeared even more impressive than we'd expected and more ancient. She was the same size and shape as a cathedral bell; she wore a plain, but all-encompassing, lilac dress, with a pale blue apron tied firmly round her middle. Her face was wide and crumpled, with white whiskers, and she had only one eye. The eye was a bright, penetrating blue and it looked at us with a slightly uncomprehending glint, as if it did not recognise what it saw.

"Can we fish in the Tea Gardens, please?" I asked. She squinted at me. Then she said, "I don't like boys. They make too much noise." "We're very quiet," I said earnestly, "I promise we won't make any noise at all." "And what if you fall in?" she said, pointing her stick at my younger brother. "He'll pull me out," said Nick, pointing at me. No doubt we looked and sounded disgustingly angelic as we pleaded our case but it must have been convincing for the old woman suddenly softened.

"No noise then. Three shillings for the two of you." *Only three shillings!* We had fully expected to pay the standard charge, half a crown each, but she had obviously decided we were too young to afford it. Our delight must have been ice-melting to behold for she softened still further. She smiled a slow, crooked smile; ungainly but genuinely warm.

"If you get thirsty," she said, "I've got orange squash."

Turning under the rose-bowers and into the garden it was very hard not to let out a few joyful whoops and yelps, but we kept our word and only whooped and yelped in whispers.

Following a flower-bordered path, we walked through the garden, past the green-painted tables and chairs and onto a strip of lawn by the water's edge. To the left was a bay in the willows, twenty or thirty feet across; to the right was a line of willow branches arching up from the water, forming a long green cavern. The furthest boughs interlaced with a wall of rising shoots – it was like a chapel of leaves with a flooded aisle.

Truly, a fisherman's paradise. Everything about the pond looked different, felt different. We could have been in a different country. The charged atmosphere tangled our fingers as we tackled-up and ruined our judgement as we made our first casts. But, eventually, our floats were standing in the right places; Nick's riding at the edge of the bay and mine poised in the glass-calm water, down one end of the 'chapel'. We pulled up a couple of seats and made ourselves comfortable.

There were no anti-climaxes that day. First, we'd won the Tea-Lady's confidence; secondly, the spell of the place was as strong as we'd always imagined; thirdly, we hooked carp. The first float to move was Nick's. At about mid-morning it slid rapidly away and Nick's strike put a dangerous bend in his rod. In a matter of seconds the carp had plunged into the willows, snapping the line. The float zipped up and landed in the rose bush behind us. Then my quill bobbed once and slanted away and the carp was in the willow roots before it had gone three yards. Again, the line snapped instantly and the rod kicked straight. However, unlike those earlier disasters, we felt no despair. It was all part of the Tea Gardens epic tradition. You battled with the monsters in their lair and you were gloriously defeated. It was the custom. It has probably been happening for generations, ever since the Tea-Lady first walked upon the Earth.

As I bent into another fish, I could properly, and without fear, appreciate its amazing power. You can experience the speed of a running carp much better when you know there is absolutely no hope of stopping it.

At about one o'clock, the Tea-Lady appeared with a tray and a large jug of orange squash. We took our lunch break, sitting at one of the tables in a shady corner of the garden. Looking about me, I thought it strange that so few people actually visited that delightful spot. Years before, apparently, it had been a popular meeting place, but now she was old, the Tea-Lady seemed to have deliberately let business flag. She hadn't exactly been rude to her customers, but she hadn't been very polite either and I think she was glad of her reputation for gruff eccentricity. I don't think she would have minded that certain boys thought she was a witch. And we didn't mind if it was true – we liked her.

Back at our rods, we tried again, thinking that although defeat was to be expected, triumph was not unknown. But we were outmatched and underpowered. Our inexperience and inadequate tackle ensured that we lost every carp we hooked. Even so, when the sun set and the time came for us to leave, we were not disappointed. It had been a day of high drama and the vivid impressions kept me awake long after I'd slid, exhausted, into bed.

A few days later I just had to return. I got hold of some stronger tackle and went back alone. The Tea-Lady actually seemed pleased to see me.

The day began bright, with a constant breeze furling the willows. At noon the breeze dropped and a dark cloud slowly filled the sky. I expected thunder, but it was only a heavy summer shower. When it had passed, the garden steamed and the air became laden with its fragrance. And while the willow leaves were still dripping, my float slid across the surface and I struck into a carp. For a second I held him back from his sanctuary then he rolled on the surface and I saw the bronze flash of his scales. He lunged forward and the hook-hold gave.

There was a long wait before anything else happened. The clouds sailed over and away and by evening the sky was clear again. The sunlight filtered through the willows, changed colour from yellow to red and faded. Small clusters of flies came out to enjoy the moist twilight air. My float was just a pale spike under the deepening shadow and I was afraid to take my eyes from it in case I couldn't find it again. The harder I stared at it, the more it seemed to blur and throb. Then it sank from sight and I knew it wasn't an illusion. Down the end of the dark cavern something deep and ponderous made a dive for the willow roots, but the strength of the tackle forced it back and I drew it, resisting, to the surface. There was a big splash, sounding in that hollow like a window smashing. A fierce pull to the left was nicely countered, the fish swerved and we both altered the direction of pressure.

With the rod pounding and bucking, I worked the carp towards me. He stuck once, the line jarring against an underwater branch, but I managed to free it. Then, just as I caught my first glimpse of him wallowing on the surface, I realised something rather painful. I had no landing-net; the bank was high and overgrown – therefore, I could not land this carp. The idea of landing a fish had not occurred to me before as it seemed too remote a possibility. Now, here was a fish, rolling under the rod-tip, and it might as well have been a thousand miles away. How could I have been so stupid?

I was saved by a miracle. A genuine, fully equipped carp-angler was, at that moment, just tackling up on the other side of the willows, by the sweet-shop. He was the only other fisherman on the pond, but he had a landing-net, as I discovered after I'd yelled across to him.

"Hang on, son!" he shouted back. I heard him running round towards me, and then he appeared through the gloom, net in hand. "Keep his head up," he said, "and he'll quieten down." Gently, the net was pushed out and I eased the shining bulk towards it. Up it came, the net-handle creaking, and the carp was swung over and laid on the lawn.

"What a fish!" I gasped. "Only a small one," said the fisherman casually, and rather unkindly. What was ordinary to him was staggering to me.

I knelt down beside the largest fish I had ever caught. In the shadowy garden, it glowed luminously. *Only a small one.* Huh! The carp must have weighed *easily four pounds*. It was twice as big as the largest fish I'd caught on Midsummer Day.

I asked the angler if, while he fished, he would watch over the carp in my keep-net. Then I jumped on my bike and pedalled home with the stupendous news. Also, I wanted to get a bucket so I could transport the fish to our garden pond. However, when I was driven back in the Morris, and after Nick and Mother and Father had beheld the dazzling creature, the bucket was found to be too small. Only half the carp fitted in and we couldn't take it home with its tail flapping in the air. Never mind. The fish wouldn't have been happy in a cramped concrete pond. In the light of the car headlights we had a last admiring look, then I carried the carp down to the water's edge and let him go.

I feasted off the memory of that fish for the rest of the season and had no restless urge to repeat the experience. Quite rightly, I thought I might spoil the achievement if it got buried under other equally tremendous achievements. And, although I presumed I would spend many more days there, I never went back to the Tea Gardens, nor did I catch another carp from Burgh Heath Pond. A deadly, Arctic winter followed that summer of 1962 and when the thaw eventually came, in March 1963, I cycled over to the pond and witnessed a tragic sight. Over two hundred carp were floating, belly up, in the melting ice. Except for the colony of tough little crucian carp, every fish in the pond was dead: the wild carp, tench, perch, gudgeon and rudd. People came from miles around to see the disastrous winter kill and they were amazed to discover the wealth of life that the pond had supported. Altogether, there must have been about two thousand dead, de-frosting fish. They drifted in with the breeze and packed against the bank like a fleet of capsized model boats. The council had to dig a pit on the heath and bury them. No one weighed the biggest carp, but I'm sure there were none as large as ten pounds.

It was only later that I heard about the crucians, but I was not really interested in them. They are pretty, jolly little fish, but they were not the stuff of dreams, or at least my dreams. The pond had lost its soul.

Worse was to follow. Within a few years those two savages of the twentieth century, the planner and the speculator-builder, decided that the old village of Burgh Heath was ripe for some modern 'development'. Like intolerant dentists they rooted out the old and replaced it with something new, flashy and false. All the old cottages were torn down to make way for faceless rows of boxes that looked as much part of their environment as pickled onions in a dish of strawberries. When they had finished with it, there was no real village left, save for two small cottages that faced the main road. Their courageous owners were not going to be moved or bought out. The Tea-Lady had not been bought out either. Much to our joy, she let the speculators know exactly what she thought of their outrageous plans. But she was too old to survive the shock of seeing her surroundings and her community destroyed.

She died long before the last old house was demolished, long before the last authentic villager moved out to make way for the urban refugees. Then the local authority allowed the lovely, tile-hung, mossy-roofed cottage to be reduced to rubble.

The Tea Gardens were swept away and there is nothing left now but the willows and a silted, shrunken pond.

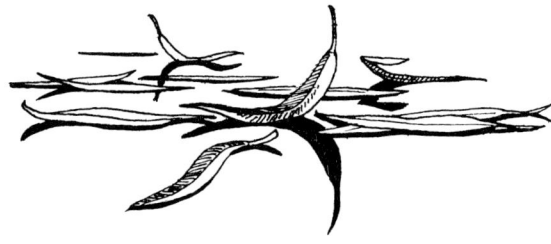

PART II

The Way to the Water

... and then suddenly there was a clearing and I came to another pool which I had never known existed. It was a small pool not more than twenty yards wide, and rather dark because of boughs that overhung it. But it was very clear water and immensely deep. I could see ten or fifteen feet down into it. I hung about for a bit, enjoying the dampness and the rotten boggy smell, the way a boy does. And then I saw something that almost made me jump out of my skin.
It was an enormous fish.

GEORGE ORWELL *Coming Up for Air* (1939)

6

A ROVING ROD

THE bitter winter of 1963 froze the carp-fisher in me and it was a long time before he thawed out. All the carp waters I knew had been destroyed and the only fishing in the area that had not been badly affected was on the River Mole. I would just have to forget the pond, devote all my time to the river and become a complete chub-angler.

The only drawback was that the river was seven miles away; a seven-mile bike-ride which was uphill all the way there and uphill all the way back. Living on the top of the North Downs you would have thought that I would only need to roll down into the Mole Valley to get to the water. However, I had to cross vales, chalk-spurs, hollows and hillocks and, like the wind, the gradients seemed to veer round so that they were always against me. Of course this was merely a form of lunacy. I was so eager to reach the river that I became exasperated by anything that slowed me down. And at the end of a long day I was so hungry and tired I felt as if I were riding home over the Sahara. It was worthwhile, though. After the loss of my beloved carp it was good for the soul to sit by a lively, bright river and let the current wash out the old dreams. I fished for the chub again and also for the big dace, which had previously seemed uncatchable, but which I learned to take on maggots, floating crust and dry fly. The fishing may not have been so dramatic as on the pond, but it was more active and demanded a more varied, flexible approach, with constant changes of technique to match the changing conditions.

In 1964 a new world opened up. I bought, for fifteen pounds, an ex-army paratrooper's 'folding motorbike' – the Corgi. On this weird but splendid little machine I was able not only to soar uphill without pedalling but also to explore the whole length of the river in a day, travelling from the source on the Surrey/Sussex border, down to its confluence with the Thames at Molesey. I discovered a beautiful stretch of water just below Cobham and, in the ensuing summers, I learnt to love it almost as much as I'd loved the village pond.

By lucky chance, on my very first visit, I stumbled upon the biggest chub I've ever seen, before or since. I'd spent the afternoon walking for three miles along the winding, leafy banks and admiring what was obviously a superb fishery. I wandered up to the top end of the water and, just above a fast, shallow run, there was a place that immediately held my attention. The water suddenly deepened where a break in a long bed of underwater lilies formed an almost still pool. Above this pool was a grassy tussock that could only be reached by forcing a way through a jungle of bramble and thorn and clambering down a steep bank. Standing on that tussock, I looked down into the deep hole and nearly fell over at the sight of a monstrous fish. Actually, there was a shoal of fish there, all chub. The smallest must have been two pounds, and there were two very big ones, the largest being so preposterously huge I thought I must be looking at pike. But I saw its gaping white lips and its black-looking dorsal and tail and it seemed fairly obvious that I was looking at a near-eight-pounder.

Within a couple of days I was back, taking a pound perch first cast and then hooking a bigger fish. As I tussled with it in the clear space between the dense lilies I could plainly see it. It was a chub and I thought how small it looked compared with the monster I had seen previously. Yet, when I'd landed it (in my new landing-net) and weighed it (on my new spring balance), it proved to be quite a respectable fish – three and a half pounds. And using that chub as a yardstick I would say that

my guess at the monster's weight was fairly accurate, though I might have underestimated it.

For two summers I haunted that swim. Never once, even at weekends, did I discover anyone else fishing there. It was the kind of place most anglers would call unfishable if they ever noticed it at all. Early morning, with a mist lying across the fields, I would chug down to the farm by the river and leave my machine by the bridge. Shouldering my gear, I'd walk a quarter of a mile through elm groves and along oak and willow avenues to the favoured place. Especially in those early dawn visits there was an almost tangible sense of excitement in the air. I had to hold my breath when I made the first cast – dropping a bunch of worms upstream and letting it swing down into the chub's parlour. Sometimes I would have no respite from that initial fever and the line would twitch and shudder across the surface as a fish instantly hit the bait. My heart would dither as the rod-top heaved over and something powerful lunged for the lily roots. At such times, every nerve and sense would lean towards what was still hidden. Then, if the fish was successfully netted, I felt as much relieved as happy and would always look upon each chub as something unique, with a quality entirely different from its fellows. Sometimes the chub got off, or snagged me. Then the sense of loss would be momentarily unbearable. On one memorable occasion, I finally hooked the monster and was smashed up magnificently. It took months before the echoes of that minor tragedy faded.

I fished almost exclusively in that one short stretch of river, and would have done so entirely had I not bumped into another angler who told me about tench. Tench had only ever been known to me through books and through the stories told at Burgh Heath Pond. Up to the day I first fished for them I had never seen a live one, only those half-frozen corpses on the day of the thaw.

Fishing text-books describe tench in enthusiastic tones, calling them 'pleasing' and 'attractive in appearance' and 'a worthy quarry'. They are said to be lovers of weedy ponds, secretive in their habits, almost invisible in the water, strong-fighting, tenacious of life. And the landscapes they haunt are usually described as sleepy, lush, bucolic: the sort of places you can still find in East Anglia and the more remote parts of the Southern Counties. However, the traditional tench country is not now as common as the more typical, modern tench country, which is the country of the disused gravel pits.

The angler I met on the river told me of a classic-sounding tench water set in the grounds of a crumbling manor house. It was only a mile from where we were standing and even before the angler had finished talking, I was tempted to dash off across the fields, rod in hand, and see the pond for myself.

I went the next day, arriving at sunrise at a gate to a wood. I followed a path that led through a valley and up onto a tree-lined dam. From the dam there was a fine view of a long, narrow pool. It was completely surrounded by tall pines, ancient oaks and thickets of birch and rhododendron. The surface was absolutely flat calm and the shadowy trees were so perfectly reflected that the pond looked like a miraculous avenue reaching away into the sky.

I chose a place where a birch tree swept low over the water. I fixed up my old carp float with three-pound-breaking-strain line and a size 12 hook. The bait was bread. After an hour or so I had a trembling bite that was hardly convincing. The quill just sank to within a fraction of its top and when I half-heartedly tightened I was surprised to feel the rod double over. The water was clear of weed or snag and it was not long before a deep-plunging fish was circling round and round under the rod-point. Gently, I eased him up; without fuss he slid over the net and I was soon in a haze of admiration over my first tench. He weighed two and a quarter pounds and seemed rather superior to anything described in the text books. A fish of continuing curves, not a straight line or sharp angle anywhere along his body; exquisite, small scales, the texture and colour of highly polished green leather; rounded fins and tail; a dark eye ringed by gold and red. He was almost as beautiful as a carp, and far better proportioned than the heavy-headed chub.

And so my fishing became a nice mixture of contrasts. At dawn I would be waiting at the placid, mist-covered tench pond; then, a few hours after sunrise, I would make a move to the gently flowing river and fish for the chub until sunset. The whole of the summer was passed in this way, the days see-sawing along with a quiet rhythm of stillness and movement. I did not catch many tench, but I always managed to land a chub or two, three-pounders being the average size. More than the fish though, it was the atmosphere of the fishing that gave me most pleasure. I remember the flavour of those summer days much better than the taste of the odd outstanding success.

Despite the enjoyment of new horizons and different fishes, these things had not completely buried my original dream. Every so often something would happen to remind me of it, then I would have to confess that though I liked tench and chub very much I still put carp above them. I kept my ears open for stories of unknown carp lakes and, very occasionally, something came up.

My first encounter with carp since the Burgh Heath days happened, of all places, at Hastings, where King Harold met his conqueror. I was on holiday with my family and, in a valley to the east of the town, I discovered an interesting-looking, reed-fringed, disused reservoir. There was a man fishing and he told me that the water held many fine carp and that, yes, I could fish there, for only a shilling a day.

"You'll find the carp will take floating crust," he said. Within an hour I'd fetched my tackle, bought my ticket and a new-baked loaf, and was creeping round the lake, looking for carp. I tossed a few bits of bread in the water and the breeze wafted them into a reedy bay. I waited a few moments, then noticed a vague ruffling of the surface film. There was a movement like a shadowy face seen passing a dark window. Then my jaw dropped as a great fish rose from the depths and cruised serenely into the bay. It circled the crusts, then broke surface and a cavernous mouth engulfed the offerings.

After beholding such an apparition, I became partially insane, torn between two contradictory emotions – fear and desire. It was difficult enough threading the line through the rod rings, let alone tying knots. Eventually, having mis-tied the hook half a dozen times, and having actually paused so that I could marvel at the way my hands were shaking, I baited with a large piece of crust and cast out into the bay. As I waited uncomfortably – not wanting to move a muscle – so the fever fit left me. The water began to look strangely lifeless and my mood changed to one of impatience. Where was he? There were no signs, no movements. I waited half an hour, then reeled in; the hook pulled easily out of the sodden bread, leaving it to drift freely. Immediately, there was a bulge in the surface and a swirl. The crust disappeared with a sound as sharp and sudden as a fat-handed clap.

Being a well-read young angler, I was familiar with various descriptions of a carp's cunning, but this was the first time I'd experienced such apparent guile myself. Or was it merely coincidence? I re-baited and re-cast. Nothing happened so I again flicked the hook out of the crust and after a minute up came the fish and down went the bread. It seemed that the carp preferred to take his food close to the weeds and reed beds, refusing to touch anything in open water. So next cast I put the bait as close to the reeds as possible.

I waited, perhaps quarter of an hour, then the bread sank silently into the depths, without any preliminary fuss. The line drew taut across the marginal weeds and, leaping to my feet, I set the hook. There was a colossal splash and a golden-scaled monster rose up on its tail and fell sideways. It was an overcast day and in the grey light that carp shone like a flame. The fish made a sudden nose-dive, sweeping the rod into an impossible bend, making the line chime like a xylophone and then snapping it.

For a minute, I just stared. There was a painful blistering sensation in my head. Then I began to dance around, kicking at everything in sight and swearing like a navvy (I was never one for bottling up my emotions).

An old man, whom I hadn't before noticed, came bravely over to me. He waited until I'd stopped ranting, then asked, quietly, "Why didn't you give him any line?"

"How could I give him line," I whined, "with all those weeds and reeds around?" It was a tame excuse though. The truth was that I had been too stupid to give line.

Fishing in jungley, snag-infested places, I'd learnt that an angler must hold and haul or instantly lose his fish. Yet these brute tactics could never have succeeded with a carp as large as the one I'd just hooked. The old chap was quite right when he said it was better to let a big carp have its head than to try to stop it in its tracks. If it became weeded, patience and slow pressure would usually get it clear again.

"Let him run next time," said the veteran. But there wasn't a next time and I went home with only that burning impression of a great upleaping fish.

It was like having an arrow stuck in my eye.

7

THE OVERGROWN PATH

OVER the years I've become familiar with a certain kind of forsaken landscape where once-great estates have gradually become submerged, like wrecked ships, under a sea of vegetation. Sometimes a grand house still stands, and even remains inhabited, though it has become too expensive to keep in proper order; the grounds, though, have run to seed and the neglected woods have become dense jungles.

Like that tench pond I fished near the river, the artificial pool or lake is often the only remaining feature of a once cossetted and well-tended landscape. And there are places where the only descendants of the original estate are a colony of ancient carp.

I found out about these things after that dramatic encounter at Hastings. The incident rekindled all the old fire and the carp-fisher in me was suddenly revived. The carp and I had plainly been destined to disrupt each other's existence and I knew I should never be quite content fishing for anything else (just as a gold-prospector would not be happy mining for tin).

I would have to find a new carp water, though I was determined it wasn't going to be just *any* carp water. There were one or two popular club lakes I knew about where the fishing was well organised and the banks kept trim and neat – as prim as a suburban garden. These fisheries were the exact opposites of the places I had in mind. I wanted a secluded carp pond in the middle of an untrammelled wilderness – a pond where you would never know quite what to expect but where you would always find peace and solitude. It seemed obvious that such a place must exist, but where should I begin looking?

There were a few experienced anglers I'd asked yet they had either been unable to help or else were rather vague, albeit tantalisingly vague, hazily recalling fabulous-sounding pools that lay in the depths of some forgotten landscape. How could these men live and not remember? The only concrete advice on offer was to get some one-inch Ordnance Survey maps of my area, scan them for all the likely looking blue spots and go lake-hunting.

It seemed a good idea and I spent almost the entire spring of 1965 map-reading and water-divining. (Being then an art-student meant that I could craftily incorporate my lake-hunts with my sketching and painting.) To begin with, I was staggered by the multitude of ponds, pools, lakes and reservoirs within twenty miles of my home. There were hundreds. I decided to stick to the smallest blue spots, those waters that would be roughly three acres or less, for it was these that offered the best potential, being easier to explore and easier to assess than larger lakes. Also, it was more likely that I should get permission to fish the smaller places.

The first spots of blue to really catch my eye were a chain of stream-linked pools shown on the map to be just north-east of the Surrey village of Betchworth. I hopped on my bike and chugged south to explore. According to the map, the pools were in a wooded valley on the edge of farmland. I left my machine by a hedge and tramped off across a wide pasture towards a distant line of trees. It was a warm day in mid-May, warm enough to generate all the usual fragrant spring scents; but as I neared the trees a new smell mingled with the others and I knew I'd found what I was looking for. Heavy in the air was that unmistakable, almost fruity tang of a weedy, reedy pond. I began to walk a little faster, wondering what the place would look like and whether I would see signs of fishy life. Plunging into the trees, I glimpsed a flash of sunlit water. Then I saw a bed of half-grown reeds and, beyond it, some partly submerged fallen trees and a vast lily bed, the leaves just unfurling. The pond was wedge-shaped, a little over an acre in extent, completely reed-fringed, muddy and shallow.

I walked up the tree-hung valley and discovered one of the other pools in an even more overgrown state. There was a crumbling dam and merely one narrow strip of water, only a few inches deep, between a forest of advancing reed-mace. Above that second pool were the shrunken remains

of a third, just a marshy hollow, a haven for frogs and grass snakes. A century earlier these had been a string of sparkling ornamental pools, all fed by the same stream. The stream still flowed and I followed it below the outfall of the lower pool, where it meandered away into an impenetrable wood.

Were there any fish still living in the one partially clear pond? I climbed a tree and spent some time peering into the water, but I saw nothing stir. Looking across the pool I could see a white domed roof amongst the tree-tops. Closer inspection showed it to be the remains of an ice-house. On the edge of the trees was a crumbling Baroque-style manor. It looked haunted.

It was very curious that the first place I explored was an almost exact replica of my imagined paradise. The landscape was perfect, like the abandoned set of a deserted theatre. However, life had deserted the ponds as well as the manor house. There was nothing left to fish for.

My second lake-hunt took me across Surrey and into Sussex, tracking down various remote, overgrown waters. One or two, though they looked promising on the map, turned out to be Ordnance Survey mirages – they did not exist. Perhaps, years ago, deep water reflected the sky at those places, but now there is nothing but reeds, willows and alders.

The best lake of the day was the last on my list – a largish water near the village of Rusper. It proved to be another artificial pool in the grounds of a long-deserted stately home. There was little trace of former habitation, only a couple of paths that dwindled away to nothing amongst nettles and brambles, and the tell-tale remains of some intricate, ornamental stonework by a feeder stream. There was also a short flight of marble steps that led mysteriously into dense rhododendrons.

The pool covered about three acres and was very shallow, with large beds of reed-mace and a great many skeletal trees lying in the margins. Two overgrown islands stood close together in the pool's centre. I was half way through a nettle bed on the west bank when I heard a violent splash. Looking across the water I saw a wave shooting from right to left. Then, after an interval, a second wave came ploughing in from one of the islands, passing quite close to me before veering away and petering out. Watching closely, I realised that the whole area of water in front of me was gently heaving and swirling and I could see pale clouds of disturbed mud billowing up to the surface.

I had found it! There was no question about it. On only my second expedition I'd discovered a perfect gold-mine. Those fish were carp, dozens of them, browsing over the lake bed for shrimps and bloodworms. I wasn't sure what to make of the sudden, cleaving bow waves. They occurred regularly, as if a carp wanted to express his feelings by putting on a startling turn of speed.

I made a complete circuit of the pool, looking now for signs of anglers or duck-shooters. Much to my relief there were none and as far as I could tell no man had disturbed that place for years. I reasoned, therefore, that as long as I was never seen to disturb it, it would not matter if I came to fish without seeking permission, for who was there to ask?

When the new season began, I went back to the island pool and was pleased, though not surprised, to find that nothing had changed. I'd come down, after art school, on a fine warm evening and I brought just a rod, net and a tin of worms. Down by the large reed bed, near the dam, I stood and waited for a sign. The carp were moving again, but too far out to reach. Eventually, I saw a reed stem quivering unnaturally, just fifteen yards away, and I cast a bunch of worms almost next to it. Within seconds – I could hardly believe the instant response – the line was sliding across the surface and my strike sent a carp rocketing into the air. It walloped about on the edge of the reed bed, but didn't do anything treacherous. Only once did it lodge itself between the stems, but I soon freed it and after a minute or two I'd got it safely over the net. It was a wild carp, exactly the same colour and shape as those fish from the old pond. It weighed between two and three pounds.

There were no more chances that evening, but I came back a few days later and had a superb catch. I arrived early, travelling down lanes that were still puddled after heavy overnight rain; they steamed in the bright morning sun. The pool looked swollen and glassy and the inlet stream had risen to a minor torrent. I went down to the dam again and the carp were obviously enjoying the influx of fresh water; they were bow-waving and bubbling and leaping.

Out went a worm, towards a twitching reed stem, where a fish was nudging at the roots. After a moment or two the reed stopped vibrating and I guessed the carp had found my bait. There seemed to be a pause in the passage of time as the fish pondered over the worm. Then he made up his mind and the line began to tighten. There was a flurry of glittering spray and after a fine display of aquabatics a nice three and a half-pound wildie was lying on the bankside grass. Soon I had a second fish, half the size, then another of over four pounds. By sunset there were six carp in my big keep-net (I don't even own a keep-net nowadays).

Naturally I'd lost a few fish, but only one of these felt particularly heavy. It made a run for the nearest island and nothing I did made the slightest impression on it. After forty yards it sailed into its refuge of roots and bramble stems and I had to pull for a break.

I fished the island pool throughout the summer and up to late autumn, when the leaves fell and formed great rafts on the surface. I caught a great many beautiful wild carp, the biggest being a six-pounder. And, while the fishing was always good, it was enchanting just to sit there, pretending to be a statue, while the carp drifted gracefully through the reflections. It pleased me that the banks were a jungle of almost impenetrable undergrowth, loud with birdsong, alive with unidentified rustlings. And, above all, there was a sense of silent power – of life positively blazing; consuming

A brace of wildies from the island pool.

and enfolding everything; gradually restoring to nature a place – an artificial lake – that couldn't endure such power. The island pool was just a dream of some minor Capability Brown and now reality was taking over.

The next spring I returned and, as I walked through the trees on the pool's east side, I was shocked to hear a sound I'd never heard there before: the sound of voices. There was also the smell of woodsmoke. I'd not seen a soul the previous year, but now I slipped through the shadows and saw a party of men dragging the dead trees out of the margins and piling branches on a fire. Others were wading in the reeds, uprooting them, or hacking and scything the bankside bushes. There was a newly painted sign on a gate post. It appeared that my private Eden had been taken over by a London angling club.

Regretfully, I had to begin my explorations again, following the maps, checking out rumours, asking questions in village pubs and hearing about lakes and ponds as full of legend as Loch Ness.

I have a scrawled catalogue of still waters in an old, battered exercise book. The list covers a period of fourteen years, yet most of the entries were made during the year I 'lost' the island pool. There are monastery stew-ponds, farm ponds, castle moats, boating ponds, quarry pools, parkland lakes, reservoirs, flooded brick and gravel pits, hammer ponds, mill ponds, chalk pits, flight ponds, reedy meres and ornamental lily pools.

My actual approach, once a water had been tracked down, was to consider the area hostile territory and behave accordingly. Inevitably, it was on private land and there was always a risk of bumping into a landowner, or patrolling gamekeeper. I became like a poacher, for though I intended asking permission to fish, it would take too long seeking leave just to explore. First I must find the right place, then make pleas to enter with a rod. I may have been stealthy, but I did sometimes get caught by a gamekeeper and then I would have to make the usual exuses about being lost. There was also the menace of the dog. Many times I had to leap over walls and fences while being pursued by these irritating animals.

My most memorable canine encounter happened at a lovely private lake near Wonersh. I was peering into the water when I heard angry barking drawing suddenly and dangerously near. Even as I ran through trees and onto a drive towards a distant gate, I knew I was not going to make it. The drive was bordered by high thorn bushes, making escape impossible. And the gate was too far. There was only one, ridiculous hope. I would have to outdog the dog. I turned and ran back towards the fast-approaching howls, trying to feel like a lion but only thinking about chewed legs and stitches and hospitals. The dog appeared in the drive – a very fat, black Labrador. It baulked wonderfully when it saw I was running the wrong way. I said "Rhoooaahharr!" and nearly tore my vocal chords. The Labrador – it was obviously just a big sofa-dog – looked at me with a nice expression of incredulity. Then it turned and fled.

I had hoped to begin the new season at a new paradise, but the whole summer went by and I had failed to discover anywhere quite perfect. There were several promising spots, but as with so many pleasant places each had a fatal flaw that destroyed its complete enjoyment: too near a busy road; too well known to the natives; the conditions laid down by the owner were too restricting; too well tended and artificial looking; its carp really were *just* a myth.

The next season had already begun before I stumbled into somewhere truly superb. I had headed south again, going through the 'gate' villages of the Surrey–Sussex border: Newdigate, Faygate, Colgate. At a bend in a lane I came to the first water on my list. It was a small, deep farm pond with willows overhanging one side and an iron fence running round the banks. If there were any carp, they weren't showing themselves, but I did see a shoal of big rudd; some of them looked over two pounds. I flicked some bread at them and they took it instantly. I had my tackle with me and was just debating whether or not to have a cast when the farmer appeared. He didn't look very happy and sounded not at all keen when I asked if I could fish his pond. Curiously enough, he relented once I'd explained that I wasn't really bothered and that I was going on to prospect for other waters. He decided on a compromise.

"You go on and look for these lakes," he said, "but if you can't find a place to fish then come back and fish the rest of the day here."

Thanking him for the offer, I went on down to the western edge of Holmbush Forest. On the map there was a large manor house with a lake in the grounds, just on the edge of the trees. I left my motorbike in a thicket, jumped a high wall and crept down between pine trees to a dark, peaty-looking water of about two acres. There was an interesting Gothic-style lodge-house overlooking the lake. It would have made a marvellous fishing-lodge, except that it was derelict and overgrown and looked ready to collapse.

Nothing moved in the water or on the surface and there was a sense of lifelessness about the lake that made me cross it off my list even before

I'd walked right round it. As I turned to go, I saw an old man sitting on a bench under the eaves of the forest. He'd obviously been there all the time and I just hadn't noticed. He must have seen me and so I went casually up to him, ready with my standard excuse. As I approached him his hat slid forward and dropped onto the grass. He stared down and said, "It was his mother's fault." And he didn't turn his head as I walked away.

Going back towards the wall I met two more rather unusual characters. They were sitting in the bracken completely devoid of clothing, and they didn't seem to notice me as I veered away from them. It seemed I'd wandered into the grounds of a mental home.

My route south through the lanes ended up at the edge of another Wealden forest. Marked on the map was a small pool in a valley, with the forest on the south side of it and a strip of fields to the north. I located the fields, and by searching along their edge I soon espied the water, glinting through a belt of trees. The moment I stepped onto the bank I thought 'This is the place!' It was deep, secluded and studded with wild yellow water lily. After that previous, expressionless lake, this pool looked intriguing and seductive.

Nothing stirred, but I was convinced I was standing by a carp water. There is a certain atmosphere which always seems to hang over carp pools, though maybe this is just an association of certain elements, or perhaps something actually in the air — something exuded from the fish.

Trying to keep as close to the water's edge as possible, I began pushing through a dense thicket of rhododendrons, hoping to do a complete circuit of the pool. However, after a few yards I found my way completely blocked. I was diverted onto a sort of badger track, or rather tunnel, which zigzagged under the gigantic shrubbery like a path through an impossible maze. Eventually, I found myself on a long straight section that ended abruptly on a high bank overlooking a lily bed. I almost fell into it. To right and left rhododendrons tumbled their dense foliage into the water and my bit of bankside was like a balcony over the Amazon.

It seemed my sudden appearance had disturbed something, for I noticed a single large lily pad begin to sway across the surface, just a few yards out. As it swung to one side it revealed an enormous purple shadow, shaped like a zeppelin. It nosed forward and the lily bed seemed to open in front of it and close behind as it pushed into open water. It hung, poised for a moment, its back actually breaking surface. Then, tilting downwards, it fanned its tail and slowly disappeared.

I stood for a long time, wondering whether big carp possessed their own field of gravity, which would have explained why my head had gone into orbit.

Retracing my steps and discovering another overhung track that forked to the right of the other, I managed to work my way round, across a feeder stream and down to the dam. The bank there was fairly clear of trees, which was a relief, and I had a good view of the whole pool. There was a sign nailed to a birch stump which told me the water belonged to a certain Sussex angling club. I decided I would have to join – if I could. I hadn't wished to share the island pool with a club that had too zealously removed all trace of wildness and naturalness from the water. But this place, though a club water, was obviously little disturbed and I was pleased to see that the membership allowed such things as a great fallen tree in a lily bed and thickly overgrown banks with merely a few cleared pitches. This was my sort of club and I would immediately write a diplomatic letter to the secretary.

I rode back along the winding lanes, came again to the small farm pond, and finished the day with the best catch of rudd I've ever had.

8

THE HAUNTED POOL

At sunrise, on a clear July day, I set off from home and rode south again, going back to that secluded forest pond, with a permit in my pocket. On the morning before, a fat envelope had arrived from the club containing such a bundle of glories that I had to abandon my breakfast and alter my plans for the rest of the week.

Not only could I fish the forest pool whenever I liked, my club membership gave me access to half a dozen other waters, all of them containing carp. With the summer holidays fast approaching, I could look forward to nine weeks of piscatorial bliss. However, for that day, though it was still term-time, I would go absent without leave. The weather was fine and settled and the urge to fish was irresistible.

The sun was only just above the trees when I reached the water. There was still a coolness in the air and a faint mist sliding across the surface. The pool looked dark and rich with promise.

It was past the season of the full dawn chorus, yet I was not prepared for such utter silence. I expected to hear the usual blackbird or thrush, at least. But there wasn't a sign of bird-life; nothing in the air, or on the pool, or in the undergrowth. However, though there were no signs of life above water, there were definite signals from below. In a sunlit corner, on one side of the dam, little patches of bubbles were speckling the surface. Invisible in the cloudy depths, carp were feeding, truffling about in the ooze. Quickly I set up my rod, baited with a tiny redworm, flicked it into the bubble patch and sat on the bank to wait.

The sun rose higher, shining straight into my eyes. It made a brilliant spark of light where the line entered the surface film and, after a few minutes, this spark began to move, trembling at first, then shooting suddenly forward. Amazed by this quick response, I fumbled nervously and almost botched the strike. But it was all right and, in a moment, a wave was cleaving the pool. The cane bent into an agreeable curve, quivering and pulsing in the intervals between runs. It was a strong fish, but obviously no monster and I soon got it under control, drawing it in a long arc towards the waiting net.

It was a common carp, the first one I'd ever seen, and I was immediately struck by the difference in proportion to the long slim wildies I was used to catching. This fish was deep and portly with a small head and a pronounced hump-back. The colour was the same dull gold of the wild carp, but the individual scales appeared to be a little larger than a wildie's. It weighed just over five pounds.

Within an hour I hooked a second carp and I soon brought him in, a small fish of under two pounds. I had one more bite before the bubbling ended and the fish stopped feeding. Over at the lily bed, where I'd seen the 'monster', I thought there might be a chance of tempting something with a floating crust. But nothing moved for my offerings and after an hour or two, I went back to the dam again.

The sun was glaring straight down so that the light was hard and flat with little shadow. Yet as I sat enjoying my bread and cheese and a half bottle of wine (special – just for the occasion), I felt no need to crawl into the shade. In fact, I was still wearing a thick pullover as the air temperature seemed not to have risen since mid-morning. It felt more like October than July and I wondered whether the pool was spring- as well as stream-fed: that would have a refrigerating effect, cooling the water and, especially if there was no breeze, the air also.

I finished my meal and began to fish again. For hours the line did not even twitch.

At about eight in the evening the shadows from the trees had stretched right across the pool and the lily pads showed strangely bright on the darkening surface. I had been fishing for nearly fourteen hours and in all that time there had been no sounds or movements in the scene around me. There was a stillness in the air as if everything was asleep and as the evening drew on, it became more noticeable and more oppressive. It was like a heaviness in the limbs, or a pressure on the mind, and it tempted me to yell suddenly and loudly and leap about, or throw things into the water: anything to jar the atmosphere. But I remained quiet.

I had intended to fish until midnight, but I realised I would not be able to do that now. I would have to leave before dark.

Usually I fish until the last possible moment. Packing-up is always the most difficult part of my fishing day. But on that evening, with the air seeming to thicken with the shadows, I didn't even make a conscious last cast. I quickly put away my gear, hurried through the trees and stepped out into the welcome lightness of the open fields.

Truly, it was a picturesque little pool. Deep, tranquil, but also brooding and disturbing. I had never known a place give me such a sense of unease before and, after that day, I knew the pool was haunted not only by carp.

I have always had a preference for fishing alone. The solitary angler has so many more advantages than a group – even a small group. He is utterly free; he fishes when and where he wants and comes and goes as he pleases; he does not need to give notice or make arrangements or allowances; he is quieter than two, sees more of nature than ten; the pleasure of success is not diminished just because it isn't shared and disasters are accepted no less or more philosophically (a bucket of water poured over your head would feel the same whether or not you were alone). I'd lost touch with my boyhood fishing pals and I had no student friends who fished. Nick's education being more demanding than mine – my chief study was dreaming up ways of avoiding education – he had little time for his favourite sport. There were one or two friends I occasionally saw whom I knew to be fishermen, but I'd grown to enjoy my solitary excursions and I was not eager to share or even discuss my little sanctuaries. And, besides, it is always good to have a secret place where no one can find you – a true island of refuge. However, after my peculiar experience, I had a change of heart. I wanted to tell someone about the haunted pool. I was not going to admit to being ruffled by it, I just wanted to describe the place in general, how I'd discovered it, what I'd seen there.

I met three fisher-friends in a local pub and, before the evening was out, I found myself arranging three guest tickets for the following Thursday and discussing plans to fish the haunted pool from dusk to dawn. It would be the first time in years that I'd not fished alone.

We got down to the water at sunset, coming across the sloping fields that overlooked the dense wood of birch, pine and gigantic rhododendron. The pool looked like a dark moon in a green sky. We spread ourselves out along the dam at about twenty-foot intervals; the Bosun, Guy Anglepen Jones, Grahame Jasper Tucker and me. By the time we had cast our baits, twilight was fading.

As before, there was no birdsong, though we did hear the high-pitched piping of bats. No movement; absolute stillness of water, leaf and reed. We fell into that sort of half-trance, that fixed and quiet state of mind that often follows the exertions of travel, heaving a load of gear across the country, tackling-up and getting the baits into the right spot. The calm evening put us into a tranquil stupor and we sat by our rods for nearly two hours, hardly whispering a word.

It had been hot during the day and, unlike last time, the summer heat had had its effect. The air was almost sultry and it continued so into the night. The warmth gave weight to the various scents wafting up from the pool or coiling out of the woods – they smelt as exotic as a tropical greenhouse. After two or three hours, though, there was no rising breeze or shift in the slight cloud cover; the air became suddenly thin and chilly and it completely lost its fragrance. There was a vague rustling in the wall of leaves behind us and someone said: "What's that?" It was probably just an isolated current of air, but I remember that we all turned round to peer into the dark. Someone else whispered: "I'm glad I'm not here on my own." There was a crack of a twig along the bankside path, followed by another swishing sound.

"That's either the bailiff or a poacher," said the Bosun. No other sounds followed so I remarked that it was probably a fox or badger.

The Haunted Pool

We began to make weak jokes about demons and ghosts, but you could tell by the way the conversations ran that we were all rather uneasy. There was an undeniable tension in the air; the soporific atmosphere had been quietly dispelled by a mild but disturbing sense of hostility — or was it sadness? Like dozing mice, we had felt a shadow pass over, like an owl's wing. So it wasn't just me. I was glad of that. The place was confirming all the things that had been in my mind. Naturally, I had half-suspected that it was I who was haunted, not the pool. My strange day might simply have been the echo from a forgotten nightmare, or too much silence for the imagination, or too much wine, or even intoxication by marsh gas. But these things would have been relevant only if I was unused to being alone in quiet landscapes. As I said, I liked being alone. I also took pleasure in being out in the night, especially in remote places. I had not wanted to be alone, though, at night in a place that felt eerie in full sunlight. In darkness or sunlight, I had never experienced anything like it.

A week of reflection, however, had been enough to make me snigger at myself, to dismiss it as a load of eye-wash. But not now. Not with the four of us sitting through the small hours of a summer night making absurd jokes to keep out the chill and laughing too loudly.

It was not imagination, and though there was nothing specific to make us nervous even the Bosun was not happy with the feel of things. (The Bosun was a Merchant Navy seaman whose philosophy for life was to laugh at everything.)

When the dawn showed in the east it was as if a great fish that we had been struggling with all night had finally come over the net. The new day unwound the knots in the air and showed the place to be just a small, pretty lily-covered pool and not anything diabolic. We all laughed when we realised how closely we'd drawn together in the dark.

"Babies!" said the Bosun.

We re-cast our rods and began to take an interest in the fishing again. We talked about big carp and the stories told about them by the club secretary. We heaped as many words as we could on top of the night and tried to forget about it.

With four rods stalking round the pool, we guessed someone would hook something. But we didn't even rouse a fish. We worked hard until mid-morning and saw not a ripple, or a bubble, or a fleeting underwater shadow. And though we said we would return, we never did.

A year later, almost to the day, I was fishing a different lake, a jewel of a place in the grounds of yet another deserted manor house. The fishing was run by the Sussex club I'd joined and, by then, Jasper was also a member. He was fishing with me.

It was a fine, warm evening and the carp were moving well. I hooked a big powerful wildie in a shallow bay and had to wade out to keep the carp clear of a reed bed. I needed the net, but Jasper was not wearing waders and couldn't help me. Then another angler appeared, wearing waders, and he came to my rescue and netted the fish expertly.

After we'd weighed and released a golden seven-pounder, we sat down on the bank and talked about fishing. We discussed the lake, then rambled on about other places we had fished. It turned out that this stranger knew about our mysterious pool. And, like us, he had once fished there with three friends. All four of them were CID officers, Sussex County Police, Horsham Division. They, too, had experienced a strange night, though theirs was more eerie than ours.

He and his friends fished the same place we had (there was, in fact, no other clear stretch of bank where more than one angler could fish). They began fishing at dusk and, a few hours after dark, they saw a dim glow coming through the bushes on their right. They presumed it must be someone with a torch until they realised the glow was on the outside of the leaves. It wasn't, said the policeman, a beam of light radiating from elsewhere. It began to drift out from the margins, following the course of the bank and moving away from them. There was no moon, no light and no mist — nothing they could confuse it with.

It was too much like a text-book ghost to be true; like a man-sized cloud of phosphorus floating round the edge of the pool. They had a large and powerful flashlight and they shone it straight at the pale column. Where the beam shone on the bushes there was a glistening, tacky sheen — like glitterwax. It wasn't like moisture or condensation, it sparkled vividly and the phenomenon made them gasp. Then it faded and they flicked off the torch. For a few minutes, there was nothing to see, then the glow appeared again, over on the left-hand side of the pool. It was coming very slowly under the leaning bankside trees, drifting round towards them.

'No one said anything, or gave a signal. We just left our rods and ran. In half an hour flat we were back at Horsham Police Station.'

Of course, he said, they laughed and joked with the desk-sergeant. But they didn't go back to fetch their tackle until next morning and though they intended to, they never fished there again. They did, however, apply their profession to the mystery. They searched through the police records for the area and, without much trouble, they found the evidence they were looking for.

Before the First World War, there had been a lodge house on the banks of that pool. The estate keeper lived there with his wife and when he eventually died his wife was allowed to remain in the lodge, rather than be moved out to make way for a new keeper. Every evening, according to the report, the woman walked her dog round the pool, until one night, for some never-discovered reason, she was murdered. They found the dog sitting by the well, behind the dam. The old woman was at the bottom of the well.

I remembered the well, though it had been half-full of vintage leaf-mould when I peered down into it. It had been from there that we heard that faint rustling – that sigh of an isolated current of air.

9
THUNDER AND POTATOES

THE sun rose over the high hills, slanting its beams through the walls of mist. There was a distant heavy splash, the first sound to break a four- or five-hour silence, and although I could not see what caused it, I saw the incoming ripple. I baited with a big piece of crust and made a purely speculative cast, the bait disappearing into the white void and landing with a faint plop. I sat back against the boathouse wall, holding the rod with the reel pick-up open, and continued watching the seething acres.

There is something hypnotic about dawn mist, especially a really big, billowing white-out, when the temperature suddenly falls after a mild, clear night. What is hypnotic is the tremendous movement of it, while everything else is still, and has been since sunset. The slowly whirling clouds are in direct contrast with the fixed calm of the landscape. The sun, as it rises and strengthens, stirs the air and whips the mist into a silent storm.

I felt a slight vibration running through the rod and glanced down to see the line slipping off the spool. The pick-up clicked over, I swept the rod up and a fish began to pull hard to the left. I let it run for a few yards before I could steady myself and apply a more controlling pressure. There was a sudden splash as it rose to the surface. Nick heard the commotion and he came round the bay with the net. I brought the fish, rolling and splashing, under the rod-point, then Nick leaned carefully out and we soon had a lovely, purplish mirror-carp wallowing in the mesh. It was just over eight pounds.

Until the previous evening, we'd never even seen a mirror-carp. For seven years, all the carp we'd caught had been, with two exceptions, true wild carp. I don't, in fact, think we had fished any waters that contained mirrors. But in the twelve hours since arriving at this lake I'd caught six fish, all of them mirror-carp and four of them bigger than anything I'd landed before. Nick had only had one small fish, but his turn was to come.

We were a long way from our usual haunts. The season, which had begun in Sussex and looked like happily staying there, had been suddenly disrupted. One of Nick's friends, Alan Crozier, had invited us to fish 'his' lake. It lay on the outskirts of his old home town, Llandrindod Wells, in Radnorshire. We looked at the map and saw that this would entail a journey of some two hundred miles. Even for a carp fanatic, that seemed a trifle far. Since the haunted pool, I had discovered a wealth of good wildie fishing and it was going to take something fairly remarkable to tear us away (Nick had suddenly rediscovered his old enthusiasm and had been fishing regularly since opening-night).

"How big are these fish?" we asked. "Well," said Alan, "my brother had a twenty-pounder and I had one almost as big."

Two hundred miles? We could walk it.

Given the choice, I would have liked to have gone by train, but there are no more trains to Llandrindod and so we took the early-morning coach from Victoria, arriving at our destination at tea-time. The first people we encountered were speaking in the native tongue and I wondered if Welsh carp were going to seem as unfamiliar as the language.

Alan led us to the lake, a large, square sheet of water with a wooded island and bordered by a narrow, tree-hung road. There was a boathouse and café in one corner. On the eastern side, wooded hills rose steeply, lending a little beauty to this otherwise uninspiring place. It wasn't at all like those lush secluded waters we were used to, but we were not disappointed. The idea of a monster carp lifted the lake out of its municipal-park atmosphere and made it seem dramatic, almost spectacular.

There was a young angler, about our age, sitting on the tarmac path in the full glare of the late afternoon sun, fishing an area of water completely devoid of cover or shade. I, who was used to finding fish in only the most overgrown swims, presumed he must be either a rank beginner or just mad. What self-respecting carp would take a bait so far from any sanctuary. But then a cloudy shape emerged from the depths, circled the angler's floating bread and took it, almost nonchalantly. After a surface-smashing fight, a fourteen-pounder rolled into a giant landing-net. We were like the Three Adoring Kings as we knelt round the miracle — although, to be honest, Alan was only mildly impressed. The carp was about twice as big as anything Nick or I had caught before.

Our temporary home, a four-man tent, was set up in the woods, high in the hills above the lake. We made a rapid job of erecting it and as soon as the last peg was hammered in we threw everything but rods and tackle under the canvas and ran back down the hill.

Walking along the bankside path, I could see the carp slowly materialising out of the deep water as they cruised around, looking for food. I cast out a biggish piece of crust and, within minutes, it was taken. But I missed on the strike. I missed another, a few minutes later, then made it third time lucky.

Nick and Alan came along with the net, but they had to wait nearly ten minutes before I brought the carp in. I had rarely experienced such power in a fish and, with open water and light tackle, the fish made several runs of up to twenty yards. The final stages of the tussle were not made easier by the sudden appearance of a crowd of thousands. Well, it *seemed* like thousands. A coach-load of Brummy sightseers had just arrived at the boathouse, across the bay. Seeing an angler standing over a turbulent bit of water, they piled out of their charabanc and charged round to see the action. Sidestrain was difficult without causing serious injury and once, when the carp took a dive along the bank, I had to wade through the gallery, shouldering people aside with a polite "Get out of the way!"

"I didn't realise you got salmon in lakes," said someone quite seriously.

"I wouldn't waste my time with them," I said, "even if they could fly." But he didn't understand.

Eventually, with gasps of genuine astonishment from the crowd, a fat nine-pound mirror-carp sailed over the net.

Fortunately, the lake became quieter towards evening and by sunset we had the place virtually to ourselves. We ate supper in the boathouse café and afterwards, in the twilight, I landed two more carp — a four- and a seven-pounder. With the night, the scene was magically transformed. The municipal boating-lake became hushed and moonlit, strangely enlarged, shrouded in heavy woods and vast brooding hills.

The long day and the long journey had not sapped our energy and throughout the still, mild night we fished with quiet enthusiasm. The carp were not much in evidence, but we didn't once consider sleep or rest. We would fish until we dropped. Nick, after a series of near-misses, finally caught the carp that had been taking crusts from under the bank. It was not the monster he'd imagined. Around midnight, I landed a five- and an eight-pounder, then nothing occurred until that moment when the sun rose out of the mist . . .

The mist had cleared by seven o'clock and about then Nick hooked a huge fish. But his reel jammed and it broke him easily. A man appeared and opened up the café and we became his first customers. Despite the lack of seclusion, there was something to be said for a lake where someone served you with scrambled eggs and coffee, virtually on the bank.

We intended fishing until noon at least, but the good breakfast and a warming sun had a terrible effect on us. We only just managed to crawl uphill to the tent.

And so the days and nights passed. We would fish from about mid-afternoon until sunrise the next day. Then a luxurious sleep in the woods until lunch-time. We would either cook our own food or eat in the café or at one of the local pubs. The weather was set fair, we had the lake almost to ourselves and the carp were obliging. Nick, as soon as we began our second day, landed a five- and an eight-pounder and we had two

more eight-pounders that day. Eight- to nine-pounders appeared to be our upper limit, but we weren't complaining. We enjoyed some superb fishing, the best we had ever known, and while the presence of monsters gave it an especially keen edge, we didn't mind their elusiveness.

After a few days, Nick and Alan discovered they were nearly broke. Being enterprising lads, they went and sought employment at the Royal Welsh Show, down the road at Builth Wells. They were appointed parking-attendants and this meant that they'd have to hitch to work every morning for five days and hitch back in the evenings. It had a drastic effect on their fishing. My own wallet was almost hollow, but I had enough money left to last me a few more days, then I would either scrounge or starve. I was not going to disrupt my fishing by getting a job, though. I would rather have eaten my potatoes.

Potatoes had dramatically entered into the scheme of things. The carp had grown steadily more suspicious of floating crust so that, after five days, they sometimes even ignored free offerings. But then an angler named Peter Smith came along and emptied a bucket of boiled potatoes into the lake. The next evening, using a whole potato as bait, he took an eleven-pounder, as well as several others almost as big. Years earlier we had read about the effectiveness of spuds for carp, but we had dismissed the idea as being too crude and clumsy. It seemed hardly wise to go for the most cunning of fishes with a vegetable the size of a hand-grenade. But now 'Spuddy' Smith had proved that it worked.

We got the camp-fire blazing and boiled about five pounds of King Edwards. While they were still hot, we set forth for battle. It made me wince as I felt my old cane rod sag backwards with the weight. I winced again when the bait hit the water. We scattered a few broken pieces of spud around the baits, then sat back to wait.

I wasn't happy about it. Though the fish were getting wary of crust, surface-fishing was by far the most pleasing way of getting carp. It was delicate and precise; you could see the fish you were stalking; it was always tremendously exciting when a fish nosed towards the bait.

The silver foil that I'd folded over the line began to flutter and hiss and I connected with something that put its head down and charged towards the distant island. It was a seven-pounder. By the end of the evening, after landing six nice fish and running out of bait, we had completely forgotten our purist objections.

Now they were working men, Nick and Alan could only fish in the evenings. Normally they were yawning each other awake just as I was

coming back from a night's fishing and I would have to be careful then not to enthuse too much about my catches. At six in the morning, nothing would be more unpalatable to two tired workers, with another dreary day ahead of them.

"Next week we'll be free again," said Alan, "then we'll make up for lost time." (They did, too.)

Off they went, trudging down the steep track under the trees, and I was left in the near silence of a late-July morning — just a single thrush or a muted blackbird welcoming the new day. With the tent-flaps open, I'd lie back, stare into the foliage above me and think about the dramas of the previous night. The luminous grey sheet of the lake would seem to unfold into the trees . . .

I suppose I would have remained in Radnorshire all summer had it not been for a promise. Like many unfortunate young anglers, I orbited two planets: the planet of the fish and the planet of the fairer sex. It gave me a pain in the head just to think about leaving, but I'd promised my love I would be home by August. I knew I could always return in September, after she'd gone back to college. (My own college days were over and I was beginning a holiday that would never end.) It would be a wrench, but I would have to leave soon anyway. There was only enough bait for one more night. I had nothing left to eat and had run out of money, except for my return fare to London. One more night then.

The two workers returned that evening, just in time for the first rain in weeks. It was a warm, misty drizzle, with no hint of the deluge that was to follow. I said it was a good omen, but Nick and Alan were more interested in food and drink. They disappeared in the direction of the nearest pub having said they'd be back for a cast before dark (they didn't reappear). I pulled my cape over my head and ate a cold, stale potato.

I was fishing near the barge, at the end of the chestnut avenue, where Peter had deposited that bucket of spuds the previous week. I had two rods, a faithful MK IV Avon and a new hollow-glass thing that didn't handle as sweetly as cane. An hour after the drizzle had stopped, the first run came to the glass rod. But something happened to jam the line and a heavy, hauling drive ended with a sharp crack. I threw the rod down in disgust and wished I'd never bothered with it.

Just before dark, the already grey sky began filling with a lower, blacker cloud and lightning flickered in the depths of it. A short while later, I watched a shimmering curtain of rain drawing across the lake. It made a faint rushing hiss that grew louder and louder until it broke into a roar over my head. I pulled my cape round me, crouching with my knees under my chin. It was an ex-army gas-cape of rubberised canvas, completely waterproof, and though the bank was soon gushing like a weir, I remained quite dry.

Had it not been my last night, I think I would have made a dash for the tent. Conditions were hopeless and the storm seemed to be actually intensifying as the night progressed. The lightning flashed almost rhythmically, yet I couldn't hear any thunder. I presumed that was yet to come.

Around the lake were four other anglers – one from Northampton and three from Birmingham. I wondered how they were faring and whether they would decide to abandon ship before dawn.

At around 3.00 a.m. the lake darkened miraculously. The downpour had raked the surface a dull grey for hours. Then, abruptly, it stopped, leaving the lake like a sheet of black glass. Only the trees continued to drip monotonously into the margins. The sky, though, remained thick with cloud and the lightning continued to throw the far hills into shuddering silhouette.

My rod lay on a wooden platform at my feet. The fold of silver foil on the line was obviously waterlogged and I was just thinking of replacing it when it vanished. In a flicker of lightning, I saw a vague grey blur, like steam, as the line flew from the open spool. I picked up the rod and even before I'd swept it right back, it almost leapt out of my grip.

The clutch snarled fiercely as something made a steady run, straight out. It slowed, stopped and I pumped it quite easily all the way back to the platform. I reached out for the net but felt a twig or root catch in the mesh and draw it tight. It became like a tennis racket. I shook it and heard something snap. But the twig was still tangled in the mesh and there wasn't enough 'bag' in it, as I discovered when I reached for the carp. The fish rolled straight off the net, feeling much larger than I'd first supposed. There was a heavy swirl and a ferocious pull that banged the rod almost horizontal. The seven-pound line only just withstood the initial pressure before the clutch gave. Rain in the works, I thought, and quickly slacked off half a turn.

It was a long run, nearly thirty yards, and when it ended the carp rose up to the surface and leapt, smashing the water with its tail. In the quiet night, the effect was like an explosion in a cathedral. The crash reverberated all round and I heard a clearly defined echo resound in the distant hills.

'What's this?' I said to myself. And I was sure I knew the answer. It was a twenty-pounder.

Almost leisurely, he swam back to me. I grappled with the net but couldn't shake out the knot. Once more I tried to slide him into the taut mesh, but it was like balancing a melon on a teaspoon. He heaved himself off the frame and surged away, getting well out into open water before erupting on the surface a second time.

This was no good. I could never land him on my own. I let out a piercing whistle and shouted *"Bring a net, I've got a monster!"* On the far bank the three Birmingham anglers had been listening to the commotion. Now I heard the scrabble of boots as one of them began to run round the lake. "Hold on!" he called. In the meantime – and it would be a minute or two before my ghillie reached me – the carp cruised lazily in again, making great black ripples under the bank. For a third time, I groped about feverishly and dangerously with the net. A huge shape wallowed tantalisingly close. It gave me vertigo to look at it. My efforts to get it in the mesh only provoked it into another explosive fit. He made a fast run towards the half-sunken barge on my left, turning at the last possible moment then, doubling back in a long arc, he tried to torpedo me into the chestnut roots on my right. Foiled by side strain, he swerved and made another dash for the open lake, rounding it off with a third walloping crash. It sounded like the thunderclap I'd been expecting all night.

One of the 'Birmingham trio' releasing my first twenty-pounder.

The pressure eased and I began reeling the carp back again, discovering after a few yards that I'd somehow looped the line behind the flyer. The handle suddenly jammed and the reel would not retrieve or give line.

'Steady,' I whispered to myself, 'if he turns now, you've lost him.' Like an outrun salmon angler, I began stripping the line with my left hand.

At last I heard footsteps behind me. It was Mick Brown with his king-sized landing-net. He scrambled down the bank and stood next to me, peering into the dark.

"Shall I go in?" he asked. He was wearing waders and thought it a good idea to net the fish a few yards from the platform.

"No!" I said, "the line's jammed. If he panics now he'll smash me."

I tried to sound only mildly flustered, though I was verging on hysteria. Nervously, I drew in the line and we saw a dark wave appearing, bulging directly towards Mick's half-submerged net. Then he was heaving smoothly upwards and the bend went out of the rod.

"Gaw," he said, "I can hardly lift it!"

I helped him swing the net over and we carried it into the avenue behind us and laid it down. Mike had a lamp and he shone it on a pale, gleaming expanse of carp.

Having spent most of my fishing years happily chasing fish of five pounds or less, a twenty-pound carp looked fairly impressive. It wasn't just that it was impossibly large – it seemed supernatural.

We carried it round to where Mick had been fishing and his two friends, John and Roger, were ready with the spring balance. On the east bank we saw a car's headlamps flick on. The engine started and the car began chugging round the lakeside road. It was Peter Chillingsworth, the Northampton carp-fisher, coming to see what all the fuss was about. He'd heard the big splashes and said he thought it was the Birmingham lads falling in, one, two, three!

It was ridiculous really. We were so sure I'd caught one of the mythical twenty-pounders – the Holy Grail of the carp fanatic – and yet the fish was only two ounces over that weight. Of course, it was absurd to attach importance to a number on a scale, but none of us had seen a twenty-pounder before and it seemed significant, worthy of celebration. The fish was a big, creamy-flanked, bull-nosed leather-carp. We put it in a sack and lowered it into the margins until morning.

Even as I stood and looked out over the lake, a pale glow began to define the eastern skyline. The clouds broke up overhead and the dawn stars shone. It was almost time to go home and, suddenly, I didn't mind at all.

10

PILGRIMAGE TO REDMIRE

DURING my early fishing days I regarded carp as my own secret discovery and it wasn't until later that I became versed in carp lore and familiarised myself with the exploits of the carp-fishers of the day and the heroes of the past. My early bible was a little book by Colin Willock, *Come Fishing with Me*. Only one chapter dealt with my favourite topic yet that short section conveyed perfectly the essence of carp-fishing. Next, I discovered the books of Richard Walker – a writer who has influenced angling attitudes more profoundly than any other this century. His famous accounts of battles with monster carp were an inspiration to me. Apart from being a jolly good read, Walker's stories proved that with careful forethought big fish were not uncatchable. And 'B.B.'s glorious hymn to the carp – *Confessions* – with its descriptions of an England that has now vanished, soon became the most dog-eared volume in my small library. By the time I was twenty, I'd read virtually everything on carp that had ever been published. There was no historic catch I wasn't aware of, no famous carp-pool I didn't know about. Only a few of these waters, however, were mentioned with any frequency. There were Cheshunt, Mapperly, Beechmere, Billing, Wadhurst, Woldale and Redmire. Of them all, Redmire was the greatest.

Redmire Pool was the inner sanctum of the carp-fisher's credo. It was the place where our high priests had their visions and performed their miracles. Fabulous creatures dwelt in its depths. It was a place that out-monstered Loch Ness.

I would often overhear groups of anglers talking about Redmire. Their voices had exactly the same hushed, awed tones that I remembered from childhood whenever we discussed the carp in the Tea Gardens. The Tea Gardens, however, seemed a jam-jar of sticklebacks compared to this extraordinary place. Had not the record been smashed at Redmire, twice? Was it not written that seventy- and eighty-pounders had been seen there? Were there not tales of a fifty-pounder being hooked and lost? How could one pool produce so many monsters and inspire so many legends? Even if you were a heretic it would be an interesting place to visit. I had no ambitions, apart from wishing to catch a good carp now and then. I would have liked to fish Redmire, but the possibility was so remote it didn't bear thinking about; only the chosen few were allowed such a privilege. However, though I was sure I would never cast a line there, I did get an early opportunity to cast an eye over it.

I met an angler, Peter Haynes, who had recently moved to Cranleigh. He was a very keen carp-fisher and he also happened to be a friend of the Birmingham trio, so he'd heard about my visit to Radnorshire. He asked if I might like to go again to Llan'dod, in his car, for a week-end fishing trip, and naturally I jumped at the offer. "Perhaps," he said, "as it's not a hundred miles from where we're going, we could have a peek at Redmire."

Peter not only knew its location, he knew someone on the estate, so it would be quite all right to drop in for a casual visit.

We set off in Peter's Morris Traveller on the last week-end in September. Even when we went downhill, we were pointing uphill. Nick and Jasper had decided to join us and our combined weight, with a week-end's provisions and all our tackle and bait, must have totalled half a ton. Most of the load seemed to be made up of potatoes.

We fished Llandrindod from Friday night to Sunday morning and throughout that time the weather was typically autumnal; very still, rather cool and the nights heavy with mist. We thought we might have a great catch, September being the carp-angler's favourite month, but by the Sunday, Nick and I, fishing adjacent pitches, had five fish to eight pounds, while Peter and Jasper hadn't caught anything. This seemed unfair. Peter deserved the most and Jasper, who'd never caught a Llan'dod fish before, at least deserved a gudgeon.

At mid-day on Sunday, we piled back into the Morris and headed south-east for Redmire. We drove through a maze of narrow, winding roads, skirting the Black Mountains and following the Wye Valley out of Radnorshire and into Herefordshire. Memory becomes hazy at this point and I only recall walking past a fine Queen Anne house, dropping into a narrow valley and so to an elm-hung dam. And there it was, nestling between trees; startlingly small, definitely magical – Redmire Pool.

I wonder, had we been normal, innocent passers-by, ignorant of carp lore and Redmire's illustrious history, would we have given it a second glance? Would we have recognised anything unusual about it? Would we have stood in awe? Of course we wouldn't. More than our instinct for a good carp water, it was our special knowledge that gave the place its hallowed atmosphere. Its unremarkable appearance and its small size (three acres) only made it seem more astonishing.

We leant on the dam rail and stared for a long time into the deep, crystal-clear water. Down there were the legends; we felt their presence, but nothing revealed itself. We walked round the heavily overgrown banks and recognised certain historical sites. Here was the Willow Pitch where Richards caught the first of the monsters and where, a year later, Walker battled with the famous 'forty-four', the biggest of them all. Here was the punt, now waterlogged and sprouting grass, that Walker and Thomas used to land the 'thirty-one'. Here was the place where Ingham landed

Pilgrimage to Redmire

his 'twenty-four', here were the islands where Berth Jones caught a monster on crust. Here was the withy bed where Kefford observed a colossal mirror-carp feeding in the shallows. Here was Pitchford's Pit where 'B.B.' beheld an apparition that haunts him still. This must be the place where Thomas landed the first to fall to the Carp Catchers' Club. Finally, here, on a still night in 1952, where the old boathouse used to stand, was where Walker and Thomas heard a splash so loud they thought a cow had fallen in.

At every pitch, we peered expectantly into the sunlit water, but there wasn't a sign of a carp. I climbed a tree and it was incredible that I could scan half of the pool and not see a single fish. The water was calm and beautifully transparent and we knew it was meant to be stiff with carp of all sizes.

So where were they? Their weird invisibility made us laugh. "This is a joke!" said someone. And then, at last, in the shallows, by a drowned, dead tree, a great fish rose straight up onto its tail, hung for a second, and then crashed back. It altered the whole expression of the pool, like an eye winking at us conspiratorially.

We were rather subdued on the drive home.

11

A NIGHT FORETOLD

We were driving down to Sussex again, Jasper's car piled high with rods and tackle, even though it was only going to be one night's fishing. There were four of us – Jasper, Anglepen, Nick and I – and only Nick had not yet seen the lake we were heading for. However, he had dreamt about it only the previous night, and as we drove along he described his dream:

> We were going fishing to the lake in Tilgate Forest. We arrived in the evening and the sun was glowing on the trees, making the water look dark in contrast. We decided to fish a bay where a large tree had fallen across the bank, and as we tackled up we heard voices coming through the woods. Three old ladies emerged from the shadows and walked over to the fallen tree. "What a nice place to sit and watch the sunset," said one of them, and they all sat down to enjoy the fine evening. The sun went down, the twilight faded and the three old ladies toddled off into the gloom.
> We four waited patiently through the night, hoping for a big carp. Nothing happened until dawn, when a small carp took my bait. It was the only fish we caught.

Of course we laughed at him. What kind of dream was this that had the dreamer catching the fish while everyone else drew a blank? Naturally, it would be the other way round, especially as Nick was unfamiliar with the lake.

It was a fine, calm evening with the late sun glowing on the beech trees that towered over the lake on all sides. We had long ago described the place to Nick, so it wasn't surprising that the reality matched the dream. But it was interesting that we chose to fish a bay with a fallen tree lying across the bank.

We arranged our pitches for the night and, as we tackled up, we heard voices coming from the overgrown path behind us. We stopped what we were doing and looked at one another. It was unusual for anyone to be walking in the woods at dusk, but we could tell straightaway that the voices we heard belonged to elderly women. Three figures emerged from the trees, but here the dream diverged slightly from reality, for there were two old ladies and one old man. However, we ignored this

discrepancy as soon as they began to walk towards the fallen tree.

"What a lovely place to sit and watch the sunset," said one of the women! But then she added, "What a pity about this mud though." And so they didn't sit down. They turned, saw us, bade us good evening and walked away into the woods.

"That wasn't bad," said Anglepen to Nick. "Seven out of ten so far. But things will change now. You may catch a tiddler, but it won't be the only carp of the night."

Conditions were perfect and we were confident. We fished about twenty feet apart, each of us using two rods. We had cast so that our baits were spread out across the width of the bay; no carp approaching from the main lake could miss seeing them. Occasionally, one of the big ones would leap and a great splash would echo against the wall of trees. Then we'd wait for the invisible ripples to reach us and nudge the reflected stars.

Dawn was just breaking when I heard the sudden, sharp hiss of line sliding rapidly through silver foil. The line was not mine and I looked across at the other six rods in their rests. One of them was quivering and shaking. But my fellow anglers had all fallen asleep and I was about to leap across and make a strike when Nick suddenly awoke, lunged forward, snatched up his right-hand rod and struck. For a few moments there was a nice silhouette of an angler, crouching at the water's edge, his rod curved and jagging. But the action didn't last long and a fish was soon splashing in the net. It was a two-pound crucian carp.

Jasper, Anglepen and I were determined to disprove the prophecy, and it seemed likely that we would. Big carp were moving closer, bubbling over our baits, and the morning became overcast and humid. We fished until noon but our lines never even twitched.

This happened fifteen years ago. The carp are still there, but though we've fished for them many times, we have yet to catch one, big or small . . .

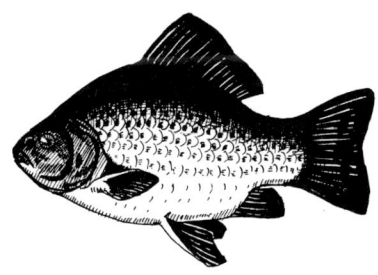

12

THE BELL AT BYTON

ON the edge of the Black Mountains stands an ancient farmhouse that two centuries ago had been a monastery. Behind the house is an orchard and beyond that is an almost perfectly circular pool – the old stew-pond, source of the monks' Friday fish. You can still see the flat river stones that the monks used to reinforce the banks. The pool covers roughly two acres, surrounded by willows, alder, pine and stag-headed oak. Though the pious brethren have long since departed, the descendants of the carp they introduced still thrive. Some of them have grown quite large – large, that is, for the true wild strain of English carp, which probably reach a maximum size of twenty-five pounds. We called the place Abbotsmere.

On 15th June 1971, we five – Nick, Anglepen, Jasper, Geoff and I – were preparing our pitches in readiness for midnight and the Glorious Sixteenth. The previous year we'd had an unforgettable night's fishing there – a night of moon, mist, carp and curlew-cry; a magical night, despite the fact that we lost a number of big fish. It was the contrast to the lake of Llandrindod that had made it seem so perfect. Llandrindod Wells, thirty miles to the north, had been dismal and overcrowded and we were driven out by an opening-day 'carnival'. We found Abbotsmere green and tranquil; a glass of clear wine after a mug of stale beer.

"Pirates on the port bow", shouted Nick from his tree-top perch. He'd been up there with binoculars carp-spotting, but now he pointed across the pool and to our left, where two intruders were standing beneath the trees. We had selfishly hoped to have the opening night to ourselves, but now our visitors dashed that hope. They began to unload the contents of several large creels and holdalls and it was obvious they were not, as Jasper had suggested, enterprising ice-cream salesmen.

Not that we really minded. It was simply that we were unused to sharing a carp pool at night. Only at Llan'dod had it happened before; on our home waters, it was unheard of. There was plenty of bank space though, and as long as they kept to their side of the pool we wouldn't throw potatoes at them. (Abbotsmere may have been a remote spot, but at four shillings for a day's fishing it was surprising how few anglers we ever saw there.)

At midnight seven small splashes broke the silence as we made our first casts. An hour passed in tense expectation. The previous season, the carp had been active from dusk to dawn and we presumed their routine would not have changed.

By first light – 4 a.m. – we five were hunched round a camping stove, waiting for the kettle to boil. Thus far, we hadn't had a single chance between us. The dawn was grey and cool and the new season could hardly be described as glorious. Then, above the faint hiss of the stove we heard the screech of a reel; one of our two visitors had hooked a fish. It was obviously going well. The angler shouted and we heard scrambling and crunching noises. It was too gloomy to see what was going on, but it sounded as if the fisher was running along the bank, trying to keep up with his quarry. Then it seemed that he had fallen over. There was a heavy thump, a groan and a worrying silence. We all stood still, listening intently.

"Do you think he's dead?" whispered someone. But then the kettle boiled, so we made the tea.

Somewhere to the north-east, the sun rose behind heavy cloud. A curlew went over, trailing his cascading, melancholy cry. The slack lines quivered in the dawn breeze and still they hadn't tightened to a fish. I went stalking along the edge of a reed bed, hoping to find something feeding. I ended up creeping half-way round the pool but there were no tell-tale signs to cast at. Coming upon the two strangers, sitting by their rods, I looked for signs of injury. Curiously, one of them had only one arm. As he leant forward and reeled up his line, his movements were so quick and nimble it didn't seem possible. With his rod held between his knees, he re-baited the hook. Then, taking his rod in his hand again, he gave a sharp flick and the tackle flew twenty yards to the desired spot – about

a foot from the edge of a weed bed.

I asked him about the dawn affray and he nodded towards his companion.

"Gwyn lost a good fish," he said. "Tried to chase it round that willow, to keep the line out of the branches. But the fish was too fast and Gwyn fell over a root and nearly brained himself."

Anglepen strolled over and joined in the conversation. It was a typical post-opening-night debate, when you bemoan the absence of the carp, discuss the prospects for the rest of the day and recall great moments of the past. We agreed on the quality of Abbotsmere and compared it with other waters we knew. The man with one arm lived near Hereford and, being a keen carp-fisher, he knew most of the local carp pools. He described various interesting-sounding places, and our ears really pricked up when he casually mentioned an old moat that contained carp 'as big as anything in Redmire'. Only a season ago, a local man had landed a forty-pounder, but the regulars did not want the place invaded, so they kept quiet about the capture.

"Can anyone fish there?" we asked, a little too eagerly.

"Yes; anyone. It's a moat round a ruined manor house. Anyone can fish it. You could, if I told you where it was."

Anglepen and I looked at each other and smiled. The one-armed man leaned forward and again demonstrated his juggler's skill with rod and line. He re-cast and we let him enjoy a few moments' power over us, for he obviously knew he had hooked us fair and square, and he surely realised we'd sit with him all day, waiting to hear his secret, or trying to coax it out of him.

Had we been hardened sceptics we would have dismissed this story outright. It was the kind of fable you often hear at the waterside, especially from the local bards. We were not completely gullible though and we never believed a story that lacked convincing detail. There seemed to be something authentic in this one – but perhaps we were over-impressed by the romantic-sounding location.

"Only an hour from here," he said, suddenly. It seemed he had decided not to string us along any further, or else he'd become bored with us and wanted to concentrate on his fishing.

"Go to the Bell at Byton. Take the road into the valley and you'll find the moat beyond an old iron gateway. Or just ask the landlord. Go to Byton, find the Bell and you'll be onto the best carp-fishing in the country."

We thanked him warmly, went round to tell the others, and the dull, fishless morning became gradually transformed by a haze of glowing optimism. The tale had all the right ingredients: a remote village; a pub; special information obtainable from the landlord; a ruined moated manor; monster carp.

"A question," said Geoff. "If this moat is so good what is the man with one arm doing here?"

"Single-handed combat with a forty-pounder might present problems," said Nick.

"Perhaps," said Anglepen, "we're fishing his pitch."

We had planned to spend four or five days at Abbotsmere. Nick and Anglepen also wanted to have a night's fishing at a craggy carp pool up in the Black Mountains. Therefore, if our informant was hoping to get rid of us immediately, he was going to be disappointed. Certainly we'd go to Byton, but it would be better if we landed a few wildies first and got back into the swing of carp-catching. After all, it would be a mistake to challenge a monster straightaway, when none of us had been carp-fishing for eight months. The shock might kill us.

As things turned out, Geoff, Jasper and I had only one more night at Abbotsmere, while Nick and Anglepen decided they would go immediately to the lake up in the mountains, a few miles to the north.

That night, the stillness was shattered by a high-voltage storm. Down at Abbotsmere, the banks shook, the pool flashed as it mirrored the lightning and the rain broke over us like a tidal wave. Yet our experience was mild compared to the trial by thunder that Nick and Anglepen endured. They spent the entire night huddled on a rocky ledge above the lake, virtually in the heart of the storm. Next morning when we went to look for survivors, we were surprised to find them still intact. We thought they'd carbonised and fused to the rocks. Naturally, they hadn't caught anything. (Only I had been lucky enough to catch a carp.)

After the wild night, the weather changed for the better. The sky was clear and the sun hot. A warm day after rain is always guaranteed to stir the carp and, as it was important to fish the moat in the best possible conditions, we decided to head for Byton. We checked the map, piled damply into our two cars and set off along a labyrinth of lanes. Geoff, who has a good sense of direction, and a good map, led the way. After criss-crossing numerous valleys and hills, and only getting lost once – at a place somewhere between Sollers Dilwyn and Dolleycanney – we entered the tiny village of Byton at about noon. We found a pub and were delighted to discover it was called the Bell. It seemed as if everything would unfold perfectly now we'd proved the first part of the tale.

We went in for a pint and something to eat and as the landlord drew the ale we asked him about the moat.

"Moat?" he said, looking at us dubiously and making our hearts wilt. "There *is* a moat nearby, but I don't know if it's the one you're looking for – it's full of branches and rubble."

"Are there any carp in it?"

"Well," he said, passing us our glasses, "there *may* be, but I couldn't say f'sure."

That '*may* be' was good enough. We weren't able to order any lunch and I don't think we even finished our beer. We bade a hurried farewell, jumped back into our vehicles and drove towards the carp-fisher's dream.

We followed a lane that led us down into a valley and directly to the ruined manor, though all we could see of it was a few crumbling stone walls beyond a set of rusted iron gates. We fell out of the cars and, leaving the doors open, galloped up the high grassy bank that overlooked the moat.

Our combined expressions as we peered into six inches of stagnant water must have been wonderful to behold.

"The old rascal!" said Jasper.

13

OAKWATER EPITAPH

In August 1971 Tom Mintram — an angler with a lifetime's experience of carp and carp waters — told me about a small pool near Bletchingly in Surrey. A few years before, Tom and his son, Mike, had leased this water from a farmer and though they did not catch anything outstanding, they had seen one or two quite large carp, possibly twenty-pounders. Tom showed me the pool's position on the map and, always keen to make a new addition to my 'water-log', I went off to explore.

At a place called Pendel Ho, I left my motorbike leaning against a fence, followed a rough track that skirted a wood and climbed a slope that overlooked the pool. It lay in a fold in the hills, with beech woods to the north and south. The water was sapphire-coloured in the evening light, and the trunks of the ancient bankside oaks looked like columns of stone. It was love at first sight.

I went straight off to find the farmer and he told me that no one had fished Oakwater since June. For ten pounds, I could have a month's permit.

Ten pounds seemed rather excessive at the time, but I thought I could ease the pain by involving someone else. And so it was that Jasper and I arrived at Oakwater on the first evening of September. We quietly prepared our pitches for the night, Jasper on the east bank, me on the west.

Making your first cast into unfamiliar water is a bit like opening a locked door to a mysterious room. Who knows what you'll find? I'd already looked through the window of this room. On that first visit I'd seen a dark shadow drifting by the edge of a reed bed. Later on, I knocked on the door. The pool had been glass calm and I kicked hard on the bank and watched the water erupt. Ten yards out, three bow waves swerved down to the dam and the surface took five minutes to smooth itself again. Now, in the twilight, I thought of my line as a torch-beam slanting into a dark corner. I was standing at the open door, holding the torch and saying "Is anyone there?"

Behind me, the elm trees up at the field's edge faded into the afterglow. There were about a dozen bullocks in the field and, an hour after dark, I became an unwitting member of the herd. The cattle came down under the oaks, where it was warmer, and settled for the night in my pitch. They lay in a semi-circle around me, their breath sweetening the air. It was a fine luminous night and very pleasant just to sit with the cattle, watching the moonlight on the water. There were no fish, though, to disturb the calm.

Dawn seeped up into the eastern sky and, at last, the line began to slide through the rod-rings. I snatched up the rod, struck, and a half-pound roach came skittering across the surface. The cattle looked at me sleepily, obviously unimpressed.

A thin mist drifted down towards the dam; the sky shaded from deep blue overhead to creamy yellow on the eastern horizon; then the sun came up, golden. Our first morning at Oakwater, and not a ripple or a bubble showed on the surface. I reeled in my rods and went round to scrounge a cup of tea off Jasper.

The first day ended without either of us even seeing a carp, but on the second I hooked something at the corner of the dam that immediately raised my hopes. Unfortunately, I was using light tackle (the farmer had told us about a four-pounder crucian caught the season before and so I was now deliberately crucian-fishing) and it was some time before I worked the fish into the net. It wasn't a carp, however, but a near-five-pound tench. Later that same day I saw a large dark shape moving along under the trees on the west bank. It was about a yard below the surface, swimming slowly towards the shallows at the pool's head. I grabbed the carp rod, hurried across the dam, leapt the stile (landing as gently as I could) and, keeping my head low, ran in a wide arc up the bank. I sidled behind a big oak and peered round the trunk. The fish was still visible, ghosting gently along beneath the overhanging branches. It was going to sail right past me. I baited with a bunch of brandlings, flicked the line ten feet out and held my breath.

As the fish drew nearer, its detail gradually became visible. It was a common carp and the criss-cross pattern of its scaling shone vividly. I was reminded of a fish I'd seen years before, in the lily bed at the haunted pool. They were both the same size and proportion – small-headed broad-backed carp of around fifteen pounds. I actually saw its eye swivel and glint as it drew level with me. Had it seen the bait? The pectorals opened wide and it hung for a moment, like a ship at anchor. It seemed about to turn round, then it just tilted downwards and sank from sight. I was left, nervously leaning against the tree, staring like an idiot. For a frozen moment the line lay slack on the surface, then it gave a jerk and began to slide away. I braced myself for the arm-wrenching power-burst, waited until the last possible moment and then struck. A six-inch perch came wriggling into the air. It was such a debunking surprise that I fell about laughing. It was Oakwater sticking her tongue out at me.

Early days, I thought. I had all September to catch that carp, or one bigger. And it was true: I did have *all* September. Since leaving art school, two years previously, I had been perfecting an Ideal Routine, which was to go fishing whenever I chose and only work when it rained. I'd realised, just in time, that careers and ambitions were all right for people who became bored easily, but for someone like me, for whom there are never enough hours in the day, or night, time is of the essence. Any fool can make money, but show me someone who can make a moment.

Oakwater was my Harvest Festival and whenever I fished for the tench or the crucians or the roach, I had good sport. Jasper had other things on his mind besides fishing, so he didn't appear very often and for most of the month I had the place to myself. Occasionally, though, when the weather was especially fine, we would arrange for all our friends to come down to the pool. Then, with a few bottles of wine and a creel full of pies and fruit, it would be more of a celebration than a quiet day's fishing. We celebrated, in turn, the autumn, Battle of Britain Day, Jasper's new girl-friend, the kingfishers and the farmer's dog. I hoped there'd be a time when we celebrated an Oakwater carp, but the weeks went by and I still hadn't hooked one.

Had I only known what I was to discover the next season, then I'm convinced I would have caught almost every carp in the pool. However I wasn't at the time experimental enough: I had faith in the standard methods and the standard baits. I clung to the old lore and waited patiently, while the sun rose and set and the moon went through its phases. Eventually, though, I got desperate and had to go elsewhere to catch my September carp. I took a few days off, visiting one or two of the other local carp waters. Fortunately, the fish in these places conformed to tradition and I was able to catch a dozen, from five to fourteen pounds, without difficulty. But it was predictable, undemanding fishing; just one unpredictable Oakwater carp would have given me more satisfaction.

On the last evening of the month I came again to Oakwater, arriving just before sunset, just before the full moon rose. I fished from the dam, dropping my baits among a scattering of free offerings that lay close to the dam wall, under an overhanging alder. As I made myself comfortable for the night, a heron sailed over and landed in the top of an oak tree on the west bank. Soon after, one of the pool's resident kingfishers flew down from the shallows and perched on the lowest branch of the same tree. And so there were three fishers watching the pool, two professionals and one amateur.

The moon rose, the colour of primrose, and the light faded quickly in the west – quicker than at the beginning of the month. The sky remained clear, but there was none of the expected mist that so often rises to chill the bones on autumn nights.

After an hour, the tench began to feed and I was kept busy until almost midnight. Then all activity ceased and there followed a long period of absolute stillness and silence. I felt the air grow cooler. The cloudy silhouettes of the oaks were becoming hazy and indistinct. A mist was rising.

The moon remained almost fiercely bright and in its light I clearly saw the line moving through the rod-rings even before I heard the rustle of the foil indicator. I struck and immediately the clutch on my old Allcocks reel began to sing, startling the moorhens and making them cluck in alarm. The bait had been lying at a depth of about four feet, yet within seconds the water heaved and broke. A silver-crested bow wave arrowed up the pool, disappearing suddenly under the misty shadows of the oaks.

It seemed too good to be true. A carp on the last night! I managed

to slow and stop it (or had the fish simply run the complete length of the pool?) and for a minute the rod was locked in a fairly dangerous bend. But then the cane catapulted back. No, he hadn't thrown the hook, he'd made a sudden return down the pool and I only just wound fast enough to stay with him. After a minute, the rod-point began veering to the right. The fish had remembered something that I hadn't. Jutting up from the shallow water in the corner of the dam were some ancient wooden pilings and the cunning beast was on a direct line with them. In a flash I twigged his strategy – but it was too late. Even as I laid on the sidestrain I felt a grating sensation, as nasty as biting a coal sandwich, and the line jammed, then broke. If nothing else, it was a perfect tragedy.

The pool heaved in the aftermath of the battle and it took a while before the broken bits of moon re-formed on a still surface. I re-tackled and re-cast, but I knew it was hopeless. Everything in Oakwater had its ears pricked and the carp, who see through their skins, would be strung taut for the slightest vibration. After two hours I reeled in and packed up.

My last view of Oakwater, from the top of the slope, was like looking down into a valley of white silk. Only the tree-tops were visible above the level layer of mist.

Oakwater was one of the loveliest places I'd ever fished and I hoped I'd be able to come back to it. Yet though I did return the next spring, I never saw the pool again. I hadn't gone blind. The blindness was elsewhere.

It was May when I leant my bike against the rail fence again and set off on foot along the overgrown track. Skirting the edge of the wood (it was full of bluebells), I noticed a strange absence of familiar landmarks. The big trees at the lower end of the valley were all gone. I began to run up the sloping field that overlooked the water. But there was no water. There were no oaks. The beech wood that had stood below the dam had disappeared. In the valley, on this late spring day, every green thing had been broken and destroyed. There was a colossal machine, the size of a house, that had dragged itself all the way from the northern horizon and split the landscape in two.

Of course I'd heard rumours, but I'd hoped it would never actually happen, that enough people would stop it from happening. The truth of the rumour was staring me in the face.

Oakwater and its valley had been one of those rare backwaters where all the traditional elements of the Southern English landscape were contained in the space of a few hundred acres. It had been neatly gouged out of existence – and for what? For the materialist's dream. For a cheap tradesman's whim. So that motor traffic could get down to Gatwick and Brighton nearly as quickly as the train.

If you have to use the M23, when you reach a spot about two miles north-west of Bletchingly think of Oakwater as just a dampness in the strata beneath you. Remember it. Sacrificed, like too many other beautiful places, for your convenience.

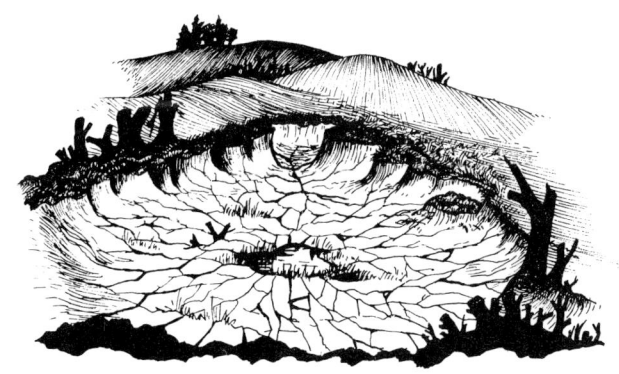

PART III

Redmire

Our long vigil had begun. It continued until daybreak, and after. The sun rose deep orange, its beams making the lake steam. Nothing moved; I was lost in a quiet world of green and grey and gold.

RICHARD WALKER *Walker's Pitch* (1959)

14
A VILLAGE CRICKET MENTALITY

On 25th June 1972, I piled a week's provisions and all my tackle into the back of a battered old Renault and, with Jasper and Nick leading the way in a Ford (they had the map), I drove to Redmire. At the gateway to that famous place we solemnly shook hands.

"Good luck," they said, as if I was going to war. I waved them off as they drove westwards – heading for Llandrindod again.

It seemed unfair that I should be the only one privileged enough to enter into paradise. As I did so, crossing the cattle-grid and following the long narrow drive to the pool, I felt almost guilty. But the feeling soon passed. The track swung to the right, past a stone cottage and along the edge of a shallow valley. I caught a glimpse of water between tall trees.

After I'd first read about it, twelve years before, Redmire had smouldered in my imagination. My first, unofficial, visit in 1969 had fanned the sparks into flames, for it was only by standing on the banks and actually looking at the water that I could appreciate its strangeness. It was fantastic that such a small, insignificant-looking pond had produced so many monstrous fish. The pool's fabled giants were among the largest in Europe and there was, almost certainly, no other still water in the world that supported such a concentration of big carp in so small an area. This double mystery of unique quantity and quality has baffled everyone and given rise to numerous far-fetched theories. Apart from the fact that the water is pure and rich in natural food there really isn't any one remarkable thing about the pool itself. There just appears to be the perfect combination of circumstances for growing big carp.

I had been thinking of my first official visit to Redmire in much the same light as a village cricketer thinks about Lords: he dreams about wielding a bat at a Test match, but never believes it will actually happen. But what if it *does* happen? What if he suddenly finds himself setting out from the Lords pavilion, bat in hand? The pitch is in view and as he approaches he thinks, You old phoney. Now you're going to get your head bowled off!

Despite my few years' experience, I wasn't really qualified for this sort

A Village Cricket Mentality

of level. Compared to the real experts, who seemed to catch half a dozen twenty-pounders every season, I was still just a gudgeon-snatcher. I felt I'd deceived Tom Mintram, who had so kindly introduced me to the head of the Redmire syndicate, Jack Hilton. And I felt I'd hoodwinked Jack, who had so generously invited me to join the group, there being an unexpected vacancy. Now, as I rolled down the grassy slope to the waterside, I guessed they'd soon be calling me the Redmire Lampoon.

There was another car parked by the bankside trees, a road-weary Morris Traveller. Its owner was sitting on the dam, apparently mesmerised. He got up when he saw me and we introduced ourselves. He was Rod Hutchinson, from Lincolnshire, also here for his first Redmire cast. Not long after we shook hands a great carp crashed on the surface, twenty yards out, causing us to instantly forget one another. We gaped, and as we stood in silence, watching the ripples subside, I knew Rod was as spellbound as I.

We had a tour of inspection and, as I walked round the banks, I felt conscious of all the triumphs, disasters, dramas and tensions that had been charging the atmosphere for a generation. Rod climbed the old weeping willow and from his vantage point spotted some fish. I swung up into the tree and looked across the water. In the centre of the pool, hanging just below the surface, were about a dozen black-looking carp, all pointing in the same direction, like a shoal of chub in mid-river. The wind was easterly, blowing down to the dam, and these carp all pointed against it, facing up the pool. Yet though they looked alert and poised, they did not move or alter their positions. I think they were all over twenty pounds.

Evening drew on and we prepared our pitches. I set up three rods, but hesitated before I cast. They were down there, those miraculous creatures. As the water darkened the monsters would emerge from their deep hiding places and range about, looking for food. What would I do if one picked my bait? The thought made the hairs bristle on the back of my neck.

My first night at Redmire and the wind was restless. I was pitched under the oaks in the south-east corner, fishing a narrow gap between two tree-trunks. The heavy foliage shelved down almost to water level and the night seemed as black as a tomb – but not as silent. The wind in the leaves rose and fell, and I could hear the steady trickle of water at the outfall. Also, there was the dull, deep pulse of the old ram-pump. At about 2 a.m. there was another sound, the rattling hiss of line through foil. I gulped. – This was the moment! The village cricketer had now been blindfolded and was about to be concussed by a professional fast bowler. I picked up the rod, paused and struck. The rod-top went over, but not fiercely. There was some tugging and I thought, Damned eel! Then it splashed, quite loudly, and I realised it was a carp after all, though not a large one. By this time a crowd of thousands had gathered in my imagination, eager to witness my Redmire initiation. I poked the net out and began coaxing the fish nearer. Something dark moved across the water. Then the crowd in my head burst into hysterical laughter. The carp had thrown the hook. Out first ball!

The light hovered for a long time in the north-east. Monday morning seemed reluctant to begin. An hour or two after sunrise Rod appeared.

"How about some breakfast?" he said.

While the bacon and eggs were frying, we sat in the grass by our cars, sipping scalding tea and relating our night's experiences. Rod hadn't con-

nected with anything, but his lines had twitched once or twice, making him jump in the darkness. To be honest, we had not expected much to happen on our first night. We had the whole week to catch a carp and as long as one of us did so, we'd count it a success. After all, it was nearly July and the rest of the syndicate, fishing the previous ten days, had managed only two carp between the whole boiling of them.

That first full day we spent fourteen hours stalking, casting, climbing trees, experimenting with different baits and being tremendously active. There was hardly enough time to eat. Monday suddenly became Tuesday and I realised why the pool had taken on such an unearthly light. Since Saturday, I had hardly slept and I was rapidly approaching that interesting state of mind which conjures such things as pulsing hills, somersaulting trees, kaleidoscopic anglers and flying carp.

"Come and give me a kick if you don't see me for a couple of days,"

I said, and crawled off to find my sleeping-bag. Closing my eyes gave me the same sensation, I'm sure, as leaping off a cliff.

Wednesday morning marked a glorious change in the weather. The cool easterly dropped to stillness and the dawn was clear, with a radiant sunrise. By noon the breeze had swung right round, blowing gently up into the shallows and tempting the carp to follow. We had read about the Redmire shallows seething with feeding carp and it seemed we might now witness the spectacle for ourselves. By sunset the fish were moving up in numbers. The breeze dropped and the water became flat calm. Looking down the pool we watched the dark shapes materialising one by one, out of the reflected afterglow, hardly swaying their tails or flicking their fins, propelled, it seemed, by some supernatural power. Those that passed closest had us twitching behind our cover like two cats ogling canaries.

At the head of the pool the water was churned to a thick red soup as the carp truffled in the mud for their favourite food. We positioned our baits perfectly and it seemed a thousand to one chance that we would *not* hook a carp. It was ducks in a barrel.

An hour into that midsummer evening and we had our first real experience of the exasperating cunning of Redmire carp. I'd seen one big fish – well over twenty pounds – nose down almost under my rod-point. I dropped a redworm right in front of him, but he completely ignored it. The same thing happened with every other carp I cast for; they all seemed to understand the trouble with earthworms. They also understood the dangers inherent in maggots, water-snails, bean-sprouts and artificial moths. Yet they showed no fear or nervousness.

"They're just preoccupied with bloodworms," said Rod. "I'm sure we'll get one, but we've got to wait till they're less choosy."

"How long do we wait?" I asked.

"I don't know. Ten years?"

Before it was properly dark, I changed my pitch from the dam to the shallows, settling down under the first willow along the east bank. With the improved conditions, it seemed the right move. Rod remained in the Evening Pitch, under the oaks, by deep water. He had a theory about the monsters' affinity with the deep centre-channel. We had a simple late supper, nothing exotic. I made scrambled eggs with sweetcorn, but emptied only three-quarters of the corn into the cooking pot. It was the most significant thing I ever did at Redmire.

"I'll just cast a couple of grains out by the weed-beds," I said. "You never know."

"Might be worth a try," said Rod, but he didn't join in the experiment.

It was a still, cool night, with a clear sky, a yellow moon and a shroud of mist over the pool. Long periods of silence were punctuated by heavy splashes as some large carp turned on the surface. I'd put three grains of corn on a number 8 hook and I felt sure the bait had potential. But after four hours with no response, I guessed the carp were laughing at it. Just after first light, I dropped off to sleep – and woke, suddenly, minutes later, to a sound like a boiling kettle. A run! I leapt forwards and saw the rod vibrating in its rest, with the line shimmering off the spool. Like the amateur I was, I didn't check myself, but just grabbed the rod and made a furious strike, snapping the line instantly.

I didn't even curse. I threw the rod down, dived back onto my groundsheet and escaped into sleep.

Some hours later, I woke to hear a wind in the willows over my head. The sky was full of sailing clouds and the sun was shining in a narrow strip of clear blue. The pool rippled in the steady blow and it looked a different place entirely from the one I'd seen in the dawn mist. Then I remembered the disaster. There was the old cane rod, lying in the grass where I'd chucked it. It had been the best chance of the week and I'd botched it. But at least something had happened. Redmire carp had never seen corn before and such a response, when I'd thrown in only a handful of ground-bait, seemed to bode well. I decided to go in to Ross and get a few more cans of the stuff.

After five days of cloistered monk-like existence, with every word subdued and every movement slow and considered, it was a strange experience to be suddenly walking through a busy town. Everyone appeared to be yelling at the tops of their voices, or chattering like monkeys. The cars and lorries were enough to drive you insane. I'd felt this contrast before – psychological bends – after long periods at a remote carp water, but never so strongly. I thought seriously about taking up a career as a hermit.

I bought a copy of the *Angling Times* and there, on the front page, was the latest chapter in Redmire's history. On the opening night of the season, Jack Hilton had caught a thirty-pounder. Rather than hope to emulate such a feat, I just thought we should concentrate on the Redmire gudgeon.

Earlier in the day, Rod had fished from the islands, casting a worm at a bubbling carp. The fish had taken it. On being struck, the carp rolled on the surface and Rod said it looked all of twenty pounds. And though it soon rolled off the hook the incident convinced him that a worm, properly presented, was a winning method, so he didn't participate in the great corn blitz.

In the afternoon, Rod went up to the shallows and beneath a leaning willow, discovered a group of feeding fish. He climbed to the top of the tree, taking his carp-rod with him. Then, from a precarious perch, he dropped a worm in front of a patrolling fish, twenty feet below.

I was watching him from the opposite bank and I didn't have long to wait before I saw him lean dangerously forward, and strike. His rod-tip plunged downwards and, under the tree, the water erupted. A small carp rolled on the surface and Rod called for the net. By the time I'd run round the pool to him, he had the fish under control. It wasn't big, but that wasn't the point – it was a carp from Redmire. I netted it and Rod came clambering down the tree, beaming and laughing. I lay the jewel of a fish in the bankside grass and the captor – a six-foot-two scaffolder and semi-professional footballer – was moved to poetry. After the ceremonial weighing (it was six pounds) and photographing, we slid the fish back and watched it shoot away into deep water. Then we opened a bottle of beer.

At dusk I threw in two or three handfuls of corn and cast a bait so that it landed just beyond a marginal weed bed. Then I rested the rod in a forked twig, attached a fold of silver paper to the line, and prepared for another chilly night. But before I'd settled down, the indicator was rattling in the butt-ring. I leaped forward, picked up the rod and forced myself to strike calmly and sensibly. The cane doubled over and a wave curved out into the pool, heading up under the willows to my right. I tried to slow the fish down, but the increased pressure just made it pull harder. I felt it must be a twenty-pounder.

The line cut into the sagging boughs, even though I pushed the rod-tip low. I had no option but to march straight out into the water. It felt remarkably warm, but was much deeper than I'd imagined and I was soon up to my waist. Leaning forward, I braked the reel as severely as I dared and, to my relief, the fish slowed and surfaced, swirling the dark reflections. Keeping the pressure constant, I managed to turn him

over and coax him back towards me. He didn't seem to object, in fact he was coming in quite handsomely, bow-waving straight into the marginal weeds. As I feared, he jammed solid in the matted, filamentous stems and I had to dig him out with the net, which wasn't easy or advisable. I got him in the end, though, and staggered ashore with a great load of weed and much less than twenty pounds of carp. I unravelled the dripping parcel and lifted out a burnished-gold common carp; not the monster I'd envisaged, yet – at eleven pounds – splendid enough to praise.

I took the fish down to show Rod and he seemed quite impressed. "Well done, old son!" he said. I put the kettle on and while it came to the boil, I changed into dry clothes. Then, taking my mug of tea, I went to watch the moon rising over the elm trees, up behind the pool. I couldn't suppress a feeling of elation, as if I'd just discovered the secret of the universe.

The ten-man syndicate at Redmire was arranged on a system of rotas, three men fishing every third week. The sydicate organiser, Jack Hilton, had the freedom to fish whenever he chose. The 'third man' on our rota was Bob Jones, who had been with the group since it was formed in

1968. Being a schoolteacher, he could fish only at week-ends or during holidays. He joined us at about 7 p.m. on Friday evening.

As I helped him carry his gear round to his chosen pitch, I told him about our week's fishing and the discovery of the new bait. However, because Bob was hardened to the obsessive secrecy of the other syndicate members, he surprised me by saying, "Come on. Tell me what bait you're really using." It was only after the next night, when I reeled in my line and showed him the corn on the hook, that he really believed me. And during that night, I'd hooked a very big fish that ran out of control, crashing through a weed bed and eventually throwing the hook. After that, even Rod, the stubborn individualist, decided to try the golden grains.

We went in to Ross and bought enough corn to fill a barn. We catapulted it over the entire pool and then sat back to watch Redmire boil. Typically, hardly a fish moved for the rest of the day, though I did manage to catch a few small fish – up to around seven pounds – from the island.

In the early evening, we gave up stalking non-existent carp and, as it had been a hot day, paid a necessary visit to the local pub. Over a few beers, Bob related some of the experiences of his four years at Redmire. He'd had an unfair share of disasters, connecting with large fish only to lose them after fierce battles. He'd taken a number of fish to nineteen pounds but, unlike most of the other syndicate members, he had yet to catch his first twenty-pounder. However, it appeared that only Jack Hilton and his comrade-in-rods, Bill Quinlan, caught twenty-pounders consistently. The average for the rest of the group was about one per season. This information, together with the excellence of the ale, made Rod and I seem less like village cricketers and more like proper members of the team. While we would probably blank with the best of them, we felt it shouldn't be too difficult to improve on the average.

The sun was still up when we returned to Redmire, but it was beginning to deepen in colour, bathing the willows with a golden light. We spread out along the banks, searching for feeding fish, and within minutes of creeping into the Willow Pitch, my bait had been picked up and my line began to trickle off the reel. I was fishing in about six feet of water and there was no disturbance on the surface as I struck and sent a powerful fish charging across the pool. There was a strip of open water, sixty yards wide, between two dense weed beds, and for a while I managed to keep the carp roaming in that open space. I called the others and first Bob arrived, then Rod, carrying his wildly optimistic landing-net (it was four feet wide). As I began to gain line I became anxious about the nearer weed bed. I didn't think I'd be able to drag my fish through it.

The water furled and bulged. I wound down and tried to keep the fish on the surface, walking backwards as I saw it plunge into the weeds. For a while it merely wallowed towards me, like a playful seal, but then it dived straight down and lodged itself firmly in the watery thicket.

For a minute, we all stood, leaning forward, waiting in silence for something to happen. But everything had clotted and knotted immovably.

The old punt lay nearby. It was half-waterlogged and full of growing weeds, yet Rod heaved it out from the bank and jumped bravely in. It drifted forward and he went and stood in the bows, holding the net, peering down and looking just like Queequeg in *Moby Dick*. The punt came to a halt exactly where the line slanted into the weed fronts. I pulled harder, felt something rise, and brought the carp in sight of the netsman. He swooped and in a moment a golden-scaled fish was splashing in the mesh. But as Rod lifted it up the extra weight tilted the punt a crucial inch. Water gushed over the bows and our hero began going down, still holding the prize aloft.

Rod's despairing expression, as he turned to have a last look at the shore, provoked an unfortunate burst of insane laughter, but I managed to recover in time. I leapt into the water and grabbed the trailing mooring-rope. As I hauled, Bob waded in and together we dragged the shipwreck to dry land.

The fish was a beautiful sixteen-pound common carp. When we'd changed into dry clothes and savoured the victory with a cup of tea, Rod said, "I never thought I'd say it to a Southerner, but congratulations!" It was the biggest fully scaled carp I'd ever seen on the bank, let alone caught, and I was quite happy, after we'd photographed it, to forget about fishing for that last night at the pool. I just wanted to throw myself down under a willow and dream. I even tried to, but every half-hour (or so it seemed) Rod would disturb me by waving a carp under my nose. By dawn, I'd lost count of the fish he'd caught – all from the Evening Pitch and all of them between six and ten pounds. (Over at Inghams, Bob had a completely uneventful night.)

After seven days, Rod and I felt we'd learnt the essential lessons. Despite the lampooning and blundering, we'd somehow qualified in the end. And despite the powerful atmosphere, we hadn't been overwhelmed.

The batting partnership of the village cricketers had amused rather than impressed the crowd, but they'd not been overawed by the occasion and they'd revealed a certain outlandish potential.

We bade farewell to Redmire. Bob said he'd be back in a fortnight, for a full week, and naturally so would I. Rod, however, lamented the fact that his work would prevent such an early return. As we went our separate ways I wondered how I was going to pass my time for the next fourteen days. After Redmire, I would almost certainly find my local carp waters rather dull and tame. As for work, I would not be able to even think of that for a while. Redmire had proved to be rather more than I'd bargained for: it was bound to become an obsesssion and I knew I was in for trouble. A fanatic does not cope easily with everyday life.

15

VARIABLE WEATHER

It was 16th July when I began my second week at Redmire. Bob was not going to arrive until late on the seventeenth and I presumed, as I'd not heard from him, that Rod would not be seen all week. For twenty-four hours, then, I would have the pool to myself. I was going to savour every moment.

It was a warm afternoon, with bright sunshine and a steady breeze blowing down to the dam. For a long time I just sat on the dam rail, breathing in my favourite atmosphere and letting it soothe the heart. I made myself a cup of tea and a large salad sandwich and went back to the dam so that I could eat and drink while contemplating the water. Absent-mindedly I tossed a large piece of crust into the pool and almost choked when, after a few seconds, it disappeared in a violent downswirl. Yet was it not authoritatively stated that Redmire carp never take floating bread? Forget the old lore, here was a non-conformist! Quickly I scuttled off to fetch a rod and within a few minutes another crust was drifting in the ripples. However, it appeared that the carp, if it was still there, had suddenly remembered its ancient prejudice. No matter. I peered into the shallow water by the outfall and beheld an earth-stopping sight.

Gliding through the weed beds, delving in the ooze or hovering amid shafts of sunlight were a great number of large carp. I had never before seen so many big fish in such a confined area; there were about three dozen, ranging from fifteen to perhaps thirty-five pounds. They completely ignored bread, but a scattering of sweetcorn had them nosing down like bees on clover. As they sent up a thin cloud of disturbed mud, I crept up behind a clump of willow-herb and dropped a hookful of grains into their midst. The take came within minutes. The line began sliding across a patch of weed, visibly creasing the surface. I struck and a wave seemed to lift up the entire corner of the pool. It crested away towards the far bank; the reel howled – but then fell abruptly silent. The wave subsided and the surface was, as before, rippled only by the breeze. The hook-hold had failed.

There was nothing wrong with the hook when I checked it. I re-baited and re-cast and within a short time I hooked and landed a six-pound

common carp. It was like pulling a minnow out of a shoal of big chub. The next fish, at ten pounds, raised my spirits, but then they sank below zero as I hooked something twice as big only to lose it after a terrific power-dive. Once more the hook had failed, so I tore it off the line, threw down my rod and went for a mile run across the fields.

The breeze dropped at sunset. Evening, night and dawn were intensely silent. The great stillness, and the fact that it was my first night alone at Redmire, made the pool seem a living, watchful presence. I sat under the oaks, fishing the deeper water, and for seven hours nothing stirred, or made a sound — except once when, very close, a big fish heaved itself into the air, falling back with a tremendous crash. About three hours after sunrise, the breeze gradually returned, like a tide coming in, and by mid-morning it had risen to a steady summer wind, filling the landscape with movement and sound.

Predictably, the carp were avoiding the overspill, but the east wind was still concentrating them at the dam end of the pool. I eventually discovered a group of big fish patrolling round the south-west corner, near the Willow Pitch, and was able to stalk them from behind brambles and herbage and peer down directly on top of them. They all looked to be over twenty pounds. The water was crystal clear and the angle of light perfect. Wavelets rippled past and the carp's outlines were distorted slightly; bands of refracted sunlight shimmered over their broad backs.

I dropped a hookful of corn under the rod-tip and watched the bow in the wind-blown line. After a short interval it straightened and the line cut away through the surface. I gave a slight jag to set the hook and a bow wave surged out into the pool. Pressure from above brought the fish gradually to the top and I saw it was a fairly hefty mirror-carp – perhaps twenty-five pounds. It lashed the water with its tail and ploughed on.

I was using a centre-pin, which made my contact with the fish feel much closer and more precise than it would have done had I been playing it through the gears and shafts of a fixed-spool reel. After twenty yards of line had ripped from the drum, I had the carp plunging in a small weed bed, but I wish now I hadn't checked the first run so severely. I should have allowed him to push further into open water, for there were snags along the near bank and he was suddenly reminded of the most dangerous of them. One moment he was wallowing harmlessly in the weeds, the next he was going like a racehorse towards the remains of a fallen willow. There was a big branch that slanted beneath the water and then, after about ten feet, protruded through the surface. The carp went straight for the centre of this upturned croquet hoop, actually leaping over it. I was so astonished I didn't think to lower the rod-point and the line snapped the moment it hit the branch. It came fluttering down on the wind and neatly coiled itself round my shoulders. I felt the spray from the enormous splash.

To lose three big fish so disastrously, after two weeks of smouldering anticipation, was enough to slide me into the underworld. The July sun felt bleak, the warm wind was intolerable, the pool looked intimidating, the carp were diabolic. It was all so tragic I burst out laughing.

When Bob finally arrived I could ease my burden by describing exactly how I'd been outplayed. His response was predictable: "You're an idiot!" But he was also encouraging. After so many chances, he said, it was inevitable that I'd catch my big carp soon. The law of averages would not permit continued disaster, even at my level of ability.

Darkness was falling when I heard the familiar clanking of a loose-fitting engine approaching over the fields. In a few moments Rod had parked his semi-derelict Morris under the trees and was limping across the dam to greet us.

"What happened to you?" I asked, pointing at his left foot. It was encased in plaster.

"Broke some toes," he said.

He'd gone in to work the previous morning, but the thought of Redmire had driven him mad. A minor injury might possibly earn him up to a week's sick leave, so he dropped a load of scaffolding-poles onto his foot. However, he misjudged their bone-crushing effect and it was a miracle that he managed to drive the 250 miles from the doctor's surgery to the pool.

"I thought I might have to fish from a wheel-chair," he said.

Bob and I helped him unload his gear and he was soon installed in the Evening Pitch. I brewed some tea and sat down to tell him about the disasters of the previous twenty-four hours. Bob wandered back to his pitch by the willow and it didn't seem many minutes before we heard his sudden shout. He'd hooked a carp. I ran round to him (it was almost pitch-black, but I knew every root and hollow along the bank and didn't stumble once) and found him testing the strength of an obviously big fish. At that time, Bob was using a rod at least twice as powerful as the lissom wands that Rod and I fished with, yet this carp swept it into an acute semi-circle. It was a long time before I was able to reach forward with the net. Bob eased the fish over the mesh and I heaved it up and out. We switched on a torch as it lay in the bankside grass and a gold-scaled flank glistened in the beam.

"Superb!" I said.

"A corker!" said Rod, hobbling onto the scene.

"I bet it doesn't quite make the twenty," said Bob. And it didn't, though I couldn't see how it mattered. It was a truly beautiful and impressive-looking fish and at just over nineteen pounds the biggest common carp I'd ever seen.

Tuesday was quiet and Wednesday saw a marked change in the weather. The wind swung completely round, as it had done in our first week. But the skies filled with heavy cloud and we woke to a wet Thursday morning. At least it wasn't cold and by noon of that day the conditions were ideal. The wind dropped, it was humid and steamy with just a light drizzle. I was in the Fence Pitch, on the east bank, keeping a sharp eye open for the occasional string of bubbles, dropping my bait as close to them as possible. I was anxious not to arouse the carp's suspicions and therefore used no splashy lead; a knob of plasticine, squeezed onto the line, gave just enough casting weight and landed in the water as gently as a raindrop. Not long after 3 p.m., a cast to a bubbler directly in front of me produced a wonderful response. After a short wait, the line suddenly blurred off the spool. I jammed it against the butt with my right hand and waited until I felt it go tight before sweeping the rod back. The reel pick-up bounced off the line and wouldn't engage so that when the carp put on speed, ripping yards off the spool, my hand felt as it if was being severed with hot cheese-wire. I had to bang the pick-up with my fist before it finally locked shut. The clutch squealed for about ten seconds and a big swirling hollow appeared in the pool's centre. Out of the corner of my eye I saw Bob dashing across the dam. I suppose I must have shouted to him.

After the frightening pace of that first run, the carp became almost docile and I pumped it back so that within five minutes I saw, deep down but quite clearly, the flash of a broad flank. Bob arrived on the scene, chuffing like a Labrador, and he too saw the fish.

"Looks like a twenty-pounder," he said.

It rolled, plunged and set off forcefully towards the overhanging tree fifteen yards to our right. Sidestrain steered it off course so that it nosed almost into the bank. It turned and I brought it round in a wide arc in front of us. Without doubt, it was a fine figure of a fish, but it still seemed a hundred miles distant. It flared its fins, swayed its purple tail back and forth, but remained obstinately beyond our reach. For too long, nothing seemed to be happening. But the steady pressure was inching the carp nearer and, almost before I realised, it was wallowing between the arms of the landing-net.

It was a graceful, elegantly shaped common carp, the colour and texture of polished oak, and it weighed not quite twenty-two pounds. An interesting distinguishing feature was the complete absence of pelvic fins. This made the fish appear much longer than its actual thirty inches. The dorsal fin was as long as my forearm while the lobes of the tail were each as big as my hand.

Ten years previously I had just landed my first carp, a fish which had brought to life a childhood dream. Now here I was at Redmire, bringing that dream to life again – except that it had grown beyond all expectations. And had it ended there and I had never caught another carp, I wouldn't

have cared. I even contemplated chucking my rods into the pool and just walking away. It seemed that I'd cured the obsession and could, perhaps, now lead a normal life. But I wasn't strong enough to finish with it so abruptly and, anyway, the obsession wasn't finished with me.

After the usual rituals with the camera, the splendid creature was released from the Willow Pitch. It opened its pectorals to steady itself, swivelled its eyes as it accustomed itself to normal surroundings, then gave one sweep of its tail and vanished into deep water.

Before dusk I caught another fish, a seven-pounder. By the strangest coincidence this carp also lacked a pair of pelvic fins. I'd never seen a pelvic-less carp before and I've never seen once since.

Next night was still and thick. The dense layers of cloud above the pool seemed to muffle every sound – a good night to forget the rods and slip into a deep sleep. As I drifted away, I could just hear, over the far side, Rod casting his bait. Once when I woke, perhaps an hour before dawn, I again heard the swish of a rod and the plop of a bait. At 5 a.m. when I peeped into a grey morn, I could see Rod was still alert, sitting behind his rods, in the gap in the bushes opposite me. As the light increased

I re-cast my own rods, then lit the stove and put the kettle on. About 8 o'clock, I heard a big, slow splash followed by the scream of a reel and I knew that my friend had either fallen in on top of his lines or finally hooked his big carp.

Looking across the pool, I saw him leaning out through the gap in the brambles. His rod was low in the water and curving round to the right. A great wave unfurled on the flat surface, then a tail appeared. It lashed the water to foam, disappeared and the reel screamed once more.

By the time I'd circuited the pool, both Rod and Bob, with the net, were waist-deep in the water. They had waded well out, hoping to secure the prize before it could mesh the line amongst the bankside willows and bushes. However, the carp was plunging dangerously close to a half-submerged hawthorn twenty yards to their right, so I picked up a big stick and threw it between fish and bush. Rod's line cut suddenly out into the lake, but the carp looked ready to turn again and I thought it wise to hurl a second frightener. It could have been disastrous: the stick hit the line! However, I didn't succeed in knocking the hook free, and instead of becoming hysterical, Rod just gave me a pained look and said, "Steady, old son!"

If Rod was outwardly calm, I knew the tension must be building inside. He was playing the carp as if it was made of bone china, yet it was obvious that only the angler was fragile. With the gentlest of pressure, he painstakingly worked the fish towards him, and in the end it was defeated, but not exhausted, by sheer perseverance.

Bob hoisted the net and the fish exploded in a furious rage, but too late. Rod raised his arms in salute and sloshed victoriously ashore.

The carp, another beautiful common, weighed over twenty-five pounds. It was lighter in colour than the fish I'd landed, more walnut than oak.

After self-inflicted injury and four days and three nights of concentrated fishing, with only a few intervals for sleep and food, Rod had achieved his first ambition: to catch a twenty-pounder. Had it been worth it? The sun broke through the clouds and a breeze ruffled the pool. Bob and I went back to finish our breakfast, leaving Rod sprawled in the grass, smiling up at the sky.

16

A POT OF GOLD

AMONG the few very big fish that were occasionally seen in Redmire, there was one common carp which was said to have the girth of a beer-barrel and the potential of a record-breaker. Four anglers had seen this fish and they all agreed that it might just tip the balance over the forty-pound mark. Rod and I spent hours looking out for it and the rest of the Redmire aristocracy. We perched up bankside trees, looking down over dozens of basking carp, but two weeks had passed and we still had not seen anything truly outstanding. Regularly parading up and down the pool were scores of fish from ten to around thirty-five pounds, but not once had we spotted a specimen that looked over forty pounds.

On my third week at the pool I did eventually behold a giant. It proved to be that barrel-shaped common carp and when I first saw it, it was on the end of my line.

I arrived at Redmire on 6th August. During the previous twenty-four hours there had been torrential rain and when I arrived, the pool was soupy and very high. A reddish-brown torrent was foaming across the overspill. As I prepared my pitch, in the Fence again, the clouds were breaking. By evening the sky was almost clear. But the sunset was like white-gold, a sure sign of further rain.

The steady westerly and the low sun made the pool flicker and glare, obscuring the signs. It was impossible to detect any tell-tale bubble trail or suspicious surface movement. However, just before the sun went down a silhouetted carp towered through the surface and toppled sideways with a crash – right over the baits.

At dusk, Rod arrived and as his car shuddered to silence under the bankside trees, I strolled round to greet him. Last time his toes were broken, this time his feet were sopping wet.

"What happened?"

"I bought a stone of prawns from Grimsby docks. Should be a good bait. Trouble is, they were packed in ice and it's a long way from Grimsby to here . . ."

His car smelt like an old tin of cat food. There was a raft of prawns, dog-ends and spent matches swilling round the brake and clutch pedals.

A Pot of Gold

I couldn't offer to make him a cup of tea – I felt too sick. Sick with the smell of prawns and cigarette-butt soup. Sick with laughter.

Back at the Fence, I re-cast and had only a short wait before my line hissed off the spool. The first carp of the week was soon smashing the reflected twilight, though he wasn't anything special. We were becoming blasé about carp under ten pounds. Rod came up from the Evening Pitch to see what the splashing was about. He, too, had just caught something: an eel. It proved to be the first of many. As connoisseurs of things like prawns, the Redmire eels were in for a good week.

That night was unsettled. Clouds gathered under the stars, broke, and gathered again: the final layer was like a great lid closing over the sky. The breeze strengthened and died, leaving an uneasy stillness. I heard only the whine of a blood-thirsty mosquito.

I, too, was unsettled for even without the mosquito I could sense something that was like a persistent whining – not outside, but somewhere in my mind and just too deep to understand clearly. It was only my reason, though, that refused to understand. Instinctively I knew what was going on. I recognised something I was already familiar with. It was like a voice saying, "Prepare!" What unsettled me though was that this message was so strong. Cold logic could only laugh uneasily in the face of such eerie certainty and so I had this insane argument with myself. It was all the more foolish because I knew it was futile. I was convinced I was going to land a huge fish and I also knew that this was not going to happen until after sunrise.

As far as I'm concerned, one of the most interesting things about fishing is the way it provides one's instinct with a unique opportunity to express itself. This is especially so with carp fishing. As I wait through day and night for something dramatic to happen, the long periods of calm settle my mind and give it a clearer depth. The moon rises and sets; the sun climbs out of the dawn mist and sinks into a haze of hot colour. Then, in the middle of all this, I suddenly notice how much I'm being attracted by a fairly nondescript corner of the lake, where nothing seems to be happening but where everything seems to be leading, so I up and trot along with my rod and prepare for a big fish. Had I just arrived at the lake I wouldn't have immediately sensed that potential. Only my surface thoughts would have been active for it takes hours of calm before my instinct becomes acute. But when it *is* sharp, when it helps me understand the atmosphere that hangs over certain things, when it gives me an insight into something that I have only a vague feeling towards, then I'm often transformed into a successful angler.

Most fishermen, I think, have experienced the workings of the sixth sense, but not all of them have recognised its significance. Those two great anglers, Dick Walker and Jack Hilton, were both convinced of its importance and their recognition of it prepared them for some of their best catches. Their formidable talent was made up of a combination of skill, persistence, knowledge, ingenuity, plus instinct. In my case, a high degree of cack-handedness plus a well-developed indolence leads to a reliance on my only worthwhile quality – a strong instinct. I could never be called a formidable angler or even a very competent one, yet I have caught quite a few large fish simply because I understood what my instinct was telling me. It can seem that I've been phenomenally lucky.

A distinct but sudden shout echoed across the pool. Rod had hooked a carp and wanted help. I grabbed my net and hurried through the darkness, towards the Evening Pitch. I found him leaning out round a clump of bankside trees, trying to stop a fish from grating his line on the low branches. After about five minutes, a lively fourteen-pounder slid into the mesh.

As Rod straightened out the usual debris caused by hooking a fish in the dark, I told him about my premonition. I said I was convinced I was going to get a big fish at dawn, but he just chuckled. The trouble with Rod is that he's far too rational – a very down-to-earth character who sees most things in black and white. But then he's a northerner.

A few hours later I watched a dull glow seeping into the heavy clouds. Dawn at last. The wind rose again, making me feel weary; a dawn wind is always a tiring wind. At about 7 a.m. a grinning face appeared through the nettles behind me.

"Your early morning tea, sir," said Rod.

He'd just passed me my cup when the line ran out on the right-hand rod. I managed to put the tea down without spilling it, but I was unbalanced as I grabbed the rod and so missed the fish by miles.

"What a rotten strike," said Rod. And he sighed. Then he gasped and pointed across the pool. "Look at those bubblers!"

A few minutes before, the surface had been broken only by ripples. Now it was almost sparkling with bubbles. Great clusters of them rose up and drifted downwind, looking like marbles rolling across a table. They were concentrated just in front of me, between my pitch and the islands opposite. We had never seen anything quite like it.

Rod hurried away, soon to reappear on the nearest island, tackle at the ready. He scanned the surface, but no one area of water looked more promising than another and he just cast into the midst of the feeding fish. I re-baited my right-hand rod and, as I prepared to cast, an enormous patch of bubbles appeared about fifty yards out. It looked as if a submarine had just been depth-charged. I made a sweeping cast and, helped by a gust of wind, the bait landed a yard beyond the desired spot. I tightened the line, lay the rod down and attached the foil between reel and butt-ring.

Often, when Redmire carp are bubbling, the odd fish will roll on the surface, gaining momentum for a dive into the food-rich silt. Sometimes they leap simply to clear the mud from their gill-rakers. However, when the carp are feeding really earnestly I've noticed that it's rare for them to show. There were certainly no leaping fish on that August dawn, just the continual streams of bubbles.

The wind lessened, then suddenly gusted again, bringing over a brief shower of rain. The clouds were beginning to break up though, and there were flashes of sunlight and even a short-lived rainbow, curving directly into the pool. Where the rainbow ended were the pots of gold, lots of them, lying hidden on the bottom.

The foil on the recently cast rod twitched to the butt-ring but the movement was so slow I presumed it was merely the line tightening through wind drift. As I watched, though, the line began to trickle and then pour from the reel.

Remembering the previous clumsy strike, I balanced myself properly after picking up the rod, waiting for the line to cut up through the surface before making a solid connection.

There is a moment as the angler first makes contact with any big fish when the image of a leviathan flashes into his mind. But then, as the battle gets underway, the image fades and the angler concentrates only on bringing that fish into the net. As my rod went into, then beyond a half-circle, I remembered my premonition. But any extravagant ideas I had were soon forgotten. There was too much pressure to think.

The carp went down the pool like a sulky bull.

"Shall I come round with a net?" shouted Rod.

"Hang on. Let's see how big he is first."

There was no pulse in the rod; the bend was locked. The fish felt as heavy but also as lifeless as a garden roller going down a gentle slope. It sank into a deep weed bed and for a while I could get no response, however hard I pulled. But the tackle was powerful and, eventually, something began to lift. Great clouds of bubbles hissed on the surface, the rod came back a yard and the fish rose towards me. The sun flashed on a golden flank, then a big dorsal showed like the sail of a toy boat, twenty yards out. It was a common carp. I could see the scales, and as it turned I had a good view of it. It looked colossal.

"Get round here, quick!" I yelled. "It's huge!"

The fish turned again and plunged down, making a tremendous splash. Going deep, it headed for an overhanging tree on my right and Rod arrived on the scene just in time to save my day. He jumped in! The carp veered suddenly and I pumped it back in front of me. With the net ready, I tried to force it straight over the mesh, but the fish simply opened its enormous pectorals and hung, motionless, just ten feet away.

I could see every detail upon it; the great scales, the plate-sized gills, the dark eyes. Its girth seemed impossible and I knew it must be the 'beer-

A Pot of Gold

barrel' I'd heard about. Perhaps it was just toying with me. I could not shift it one way or the other and I guessed it might at any moment make some devastating rush. But then, with the tension running from the rod right down to my boots, it came in a few inches, then a few more.

Rod was either stuck in the mud or transfixed by the sight of the monster, for he didn't reappear until I'd finally coaxed the fish over the net and heaved the mesh up around it. I couldn't lift it from the water, though; at least not with one hand. It was too heavy.

"Christ!" said Rod. "It's a bloomin' record!"

We soaked a sack, weighed it, then put the carp in it and hoisted it onto the scales. After a simple subtraction we arrived at a figure of forty-four pounds and one ounce. But a second, more careful weighing an hour later showed the fish to be just over forty-three and three-quarter pounds.

At the time it was the country's second biggest carp. Unfortunately, once out of the water, it proved to be a blubbery, spawny beast and not exactly pleasing in appearance.

What I *was* pleased about was the way it confirmed an image which had been swimming in my head since sunset, twelve hours before.

17

REDMIRE REFLECTIONS

REDMIRE was fascinating not only because of its carp. I'm sure, for instance, that it was no coincidence that the biggest grass snake I ever saw lived on its banks. Several times I spotted it and twice I tried to catch it, but it was too quick for me. Once I saw it lying stretched across the track on the dam and before I made a dive towards it (I only wanted to have a closer look at it; I didn't want to keep it) I made a mental note of the position of the head, which was next to a stone, and the tail, which lay across a tuft of grass. It whiplashed into the water as soon as I moved, but afterwards I was able to state, with reasonable accuracy, that I'd seen a grass snake measuring nearly five and a half feet in length. An average specimen is a little under three feet.

The only other fish in the pool besides carp were eels and gudgeon. There used to be, many years ago, even before the carp, a colony of trout but for various reasons they died out. The eels were frequently irritating, especially when they bubbled. They had a habit of drilling themselves into the lake bed in their search for bloodworms which caused a small patch of bubbles to rise to the surface. Many times an angler has stalked a bubbling carp and failed to catch it, simply because the carp was not a carp. The eels were also irritating because of their great delight in anything the slightest bit wormy, or maggoty, or meaty. Especially after dark, it was folly to use such baits.

Most of the eels were only the size of a decent runner bean and it was unusual to catch anything bigger than two pounds. However, in keeping with the tradition of the place, the Redmire eel population had its own king. One day, some years after the punt had been restored, I was paddling across the pool between the Stile and Pitchfords when a monster the size of a python rose up out of the weeds below me. Had I been the only person to see it I wouldn't have believed my eyes. But that amicable angler, Roy Henry Tuckey, was punting with me and he too had a clear view of the giant. It slanted up from deep water until it was about six feet below us, then it levelled off and moved forward, looking curiously stiff and unreal. There were no undulations of its body, it simply cruised ahead as if propelled by magic. As it went under the punt the tail was visible on one side and the head on the other. One of us must have made a movement for the creature gave a sudden twitch of its tail and speared itself back into the weed beds.

We both agreed it was about five feet long (nearly as long as that snake), but it's difficult to judge an eel's weight when you've never seen a live one above three pounds. Bob Jones has an eight-pounder in a glass case and using that as a yardstick, the Redmire 'python' could have weighed anything between ten and fifteen pounds, which is a mighty huge eel.

Richard Walker recalls seeing a gudgeon that looked all of a pound, and that's four times heavier than the gudgeon record. I never saw anything like that even though I used to see a lot of gudgeon. There were times when, frustrated by the carp, I would sit on the dam and console myself with a bit of tiddler snatching. Gudgeon fishing is the perfect antedote to the emotional pressures of stalking big pernickety carp. At Redmire especially, it seemed a particularly silly thing to do, which added to the enjoyment. There I was, a confirmed carp-addict, blessed with the honour of being able to fish the greatest carp water in the land. And what do I do? I fish for gudgeon. How irreverent!

It was just pleasant to be watching an active float and catching fish again. Maggots, worms, or bread on a size 12 and a crow-quill: this was the set-up and it was guaranteed to give sparkling results.

Also there were times when the sport could be surprisingly exciting. Occasionally, as I reacted to a downward twitch of the quill, I'd be dragged to my feet by something that felt like a whale. Any fish over a pound gives you a jolt when you are only expecting a one-ounce gudgeon, but when a double-figure carp sets the reel howling, it's like being struck by lightning. This element of surprise was sometimes enough to keep me gudgeon fishing for a whole day, yet the funny thing was that if I ever began consciously to hope for carp, I never got one. I'm sure this was because the carp sensed that I'd gone off the boil. They presumed I was merely a simple gudgeon-fisher and so it was quite safe to begin feeding. Therefore the attitude of the true gudgeon-fisher is a good one to adopt. You are sure of success, whatever happens.

On one memorable September afternoon the gudgeon swim I was fishing became a mass of carp bubbles. A switch from worm to corn – which the gudgeon always ignored – produced a marvellous result. For the only time I can remember, the carp behaved like the gudgeon themselves, taking the float under every ten minutes or so and mopping up the ground-bait as fast as I could throw it in. Though I didn't catch anything huge it was perhaps the most entertaining day's fishing I ever had at Redmire. I took over a dozen carp from five to sixteen pounds. All were fully scaled and all took a single grain of corn on a size 12, float-fished in four feet of water at the overspill corner of the dam. I used six-pound line, an ancient centre-pin reel, and my lightest rod, yet I didn't lose a single fish, and the four biggest ones – all double figures – pulled like horses.

Another nice thing about the Redmire gudgeon was their tendency to buzz. On a still, summer night when you had been waiting by the rods for hours and nothing had stirred for all that time, it was amusing and somehow comforting to hear, close in, a "gudgeon buzz". The little fish, for a reason known only to itself, would leap right into the air and shake its body so violently that it vibrated like a bee's wing. But it was just a faint buzz, which was why it was audible only on still nights. For a time I presumed that carp-fry were responsible, but close observation in daylight revealed the true culprit. The small silver fish would pop up like a cork and then become just a blur before plopping back in the water. "Bzzzzzzz!" it went.

There was another buzzing I once heard, while leaning against an old willow up by the shallows. It was a deep drone, as if the ancient tree was creaking at its roots. As I was half asleep I didn't pay much attention until I realised the sound was becoming rapidly louder. I leaned forward and looked round and a diabolic-looking hornet emerged from a crack in the bark where I'd unwittingly trapped it. No, it wasn't the size of a duck, even though we are at Redmire. But it gave me a shock. The insect flew up, banked, dived and began to show displeasure towards me. It chased me right down to the dam.

The pool itself obviously has a long and interesting history. It was formed centuries ago by the damming of a small stream and its original purpose was to supply fresh water rather than fresh fish to the medieval court four hundred yards to the south-east. During my summers at Redmire I discovered some fascinating stories concerning events there during the past sixty years. In the 1930s for instance, the owners of the court arranged for concerts of chamber music to be performed on the dam. And while the gentle strains of Mozart and Schubert drifted across the pool the guests drifted with it, comfortably reclining in punts while a butler in a rowing-boat was paddled round with the port and brandy.

What charming, civilised evenings they must have been. And a point to remember is that the present population of carp was introduced as fry in 1934. Perhaps one of the reasons they prospered so famously was because of their early acquaintance with music. Carp obviously grow best when properly cultivated.

Curiously enough, I had a discussion about the carp's musical sensibilities with Redmire's present owner, Michael Richardson. I mentioned the fact that while the fish seemed to appreciate classical music (they drifted close when I switched on a car radio), they detested 'pop', quickly sinking away as I switched to a commercial station. We commented on their good taste. Their early musical education had probably affected them.

My most valued informant on local history was Jack the Roadman, a wonderful character whom Rod Hutchinson and I first met in the local pub, the Royal Arms. Jack Farmer was his real name. Jack knew the pool well in the pre-war years, long before it began to be known as Redmire (the name was invented as a 'blind' by Dick Walker in 1952). In the 1930s Jack followed an otter hunt up the river, along the stream and finally to the pool. At first, the otter had managed to keep well ahead of the hounds, but by the time it was scampering over the dam it was just inches in front of the leading dog. Once in deep water, though, it knew it was safe. It rose up a few yards out and taunted the pack. The master came up and took stock.

"Trouble was," said Jack, "he'd had a fair few glasses already. He just looked at the otter, shouted for us all to follow and marched straight in behind the dogs. The water was ten feet deep and all we could see of the master was his hat, floating on the top!" He added that he was very glad to see the otter escape.

Jack didn't remember ever seeing any carp and even if he had, they would not have interested him. He'd fished for the Redmire eels because he appreciated them in a pie, but what he liked best was the trout in the local river. Over the years, he probably caught more trout from there than anyone else in the valley – and all on a hand-line.

"Better than a rod," he explained. "Wraps up neat in the pocket when the keeper comes along." He may have been a bit of a rogue, but he was a very warm-hearted one. He also had sound judgement and clear sight. He bemoaned the loss of his friends in the fields and said, "You don't see 'em like you used to; the buzzards and hares and long-tailed tits and badgers. And when they're gone you'll know too many other things will have gone with 'em."

When Rod and I came into the pub either to celebrate a good catch

or to drown our sorrows, Jack was always quick to congratulate or commiserate or make some joke at our expense.

"Look at their faces!" he once said to the landlord. "They've been on the water so long they're beginning to look like them carp."

During a long stint it was important to us to get away from Redmire for an hour or two, every other day. Sometimes the fishing became unusually intense and one could actually sense a sort of charge building up. When that happened it was almost a relief to drive over to the pub and talk about things other than fishing for a while. Of course we *did* talk about fishing as well. In fact some of our best plans were hatched over a pint of ale, with Jack looking on quizzically, amazed at our never-ending enthusiasm. He thought, as did all the other locals, that we were quite mad. I remember, years after I stopped fishing Redmire, going back to the Royal Arms with two fisher-friends, Derby and Jan. We sat down in the almost empty bar and the only other customer looked across at me from the top of his glass and said, "I remember you. You're mad!"

"Carp-fever" was the term used by "B.B." to describe our complaint. We were passionately involved with carp and after whole summers of almost continual fishing I often wondered where it was all going to lead. I think the fact that the locals thought we were mad prevented us from actually becoming so. They reminded us of what it was like to be normal. By their refreshingly honest, deep-rooted attitudes, they defined a quality of rightness and wholeness that I've not found elsewhere. Being right out on the Welsh borderlands, away from the mindless urgency of modern towns and main roads, the locals all appeared to take more interest in real life. In the pub, I never heard anyone talking about television or national celebrities. They rarely discussed politics, even though bad politics had destroyed many small communities like theirs. They only trusted in their own experience, were suspicious of second-hand knowledge, were interested in the natural events taking place around them. Each had original, genuine character and, in their comfortable countrymen's clothes, possessed a natural dignity and warm humanity which is now as rare as most good things in this world.

According to local legend, a skeleton was discovered at Redmire, in a secret room (probably a priest-hole) in the 'big house'. This story is, I think, true, as I discovered it again recently in a book of local history. I wonder if the ghost of that unknown person is the one who still haunts the site of the old boat-house, under the oaks on the pool's east side.

I'm usually sceptical about other folk's ghost stories. Most people have little experience of the night, yet most ghosts are met with at night. Someone unfamiliar with night's undercurrents, but who walks or fishes alone at night, is often liable to see or hear something odd that cannot be simply explained. Sooner or later one of these strange incidents becomes the foundation for yet another ghost story. Yet the 'ghost' was probably only moonlight on a column of mist or the shadow of an owl or the scream of a vixen or a badger foraging through leaves. A friend of mine was once so disturbed by the 'chur' of a night-jar – which he didn't recognise as such – that he buried his head inside his sleeping-bag in fright. But while I'm all too ready to dismiss other people's ghost stories I do believe in ghosts – or at least in the idea that a powerful presence or an intense emotion or mood can outlast a life, like a cloud of mist hanging over a dried-up pond. I also believe in the different strengths of ghosts. It takes a person of extraordinary sensitivity to be aware of a 'weak' ghost, but sometimes the aura is strong enough for almost anyone to appreciate it, as is the case with the Redmire haunting (predictable, I suppose).

Most of the anglers who experienced the ghost of the boat-house were not the sort of people you would expect to believe in such things. They were also reluctant to discuss their experiences and it was only after discovering that we all had similar tales to tell that the mystery began to unfold.

One of 'B.B.'s' earliest memories of Redmire was of a 'strange stirring' under the oaks. On the stillest summer day, or in the depths of a silent night, he was often aware of that peculiar restlessness in the atmosphere. Another angler I know was disturbed by an unknown voice while someone else was so convinced that he was being continually observed by someone he couldn't see that he spent more time looking behind him than watching his rods. In the late 1970s when I was fishing with Barry Mills, Barry woke up under the oaks one night and saw a shadowy figure standing close by. There was only the two of us at the pool and he presumed the figure was me, come round to report a carp. But as he stood up the figure vanished so mysteriously that Barry had to nip across the dam to where I was pitched to satisfy himself that I wasn't playing tricks. He found me, oblivious to the world, asleep by the willows. In the morning he asked me whether I was prone to sleep-walking, but he eventually admitted that he knew it couldn't really have been me, or a poacher or anybody else. He was, and still is, convinced that he saw an authentic ghost.

As for myself, I never saw anything. But there were many nights when I woke from a deep sleep in the Evening Pitch – on the site of the old boat-house – and either heard a voice or felt an indefinable yet undeniable presence, as when someone enters a room unseen and unheard, but you are aware of their arrival. Once or twice I felt compelled to stand up and look around asking, "I know you're there, but *who* are you?"

My first experience of the haunting was by far the most disturbing. It was on a wild, autumnal night in 1973. I'd arrived at Redmire after dark and found the place deserted. I'd not planned to go fishing at all that week, but something had stirred me and I just dropped what I'd been doing and went off with the rods for a few days. I quickly dumped my gear in the Evening Pitch, cast out, made a cup of tea and then sat back to listen to the wind in the trees. It was one of those ferocious gales we often get at the time of the autumn equinox and the whole landscape roared like the sea. Around midnight the wind abated a little and I was just thinking that I might get some sleep after all when a tremendous shout echoed across the pool. It had seemed to come from the left, about a yard away, and I literally jumped into the air.

There was a fairly pregnant silence afterwards as I listened, ears pricked, for the slightest sound of someone moving over the fallen leaves. But there was no sound. I searched the near banks and scanned the surrounding fields (there was moon enough to see). There was no one, and indeed no stranger ever came unannounced to the pool, day or night.

For me, the eeriest thing about this story is that I distinctly heard what had been shouted. It was my own name.

18

AUTUMN AND A CARP TO REMEMBER

THE first frosts had come and the year was beginning to look old, with the leaves falling, the grass withering and the water in the lakes and rivers going dark and steely. I thought I might not go back to Redmire until the next summer. It had still been green and lush on my previous visit and now I didn't wish to see it fading into winter. But on the Tuesday of our scheduled October week, Rod phoned from the village near the pool. He'd been fishing since Sunday and, with the weather wet and windy, the carp had been feeding. He'd caught a twenty-two pounder from Inghams, on float tackle. But, more important, he'd actually seen the king of the pool, the gigantic common carp that was reputed to weigh anything up to eighty or even ninety pounds. Rod had watched it do a half-roll on the surface. He'd had a good, clear view of it and was quite obviously staggered. Between the regular pumping of coins into the slot, he kept repeating words like *amazing* and *enormous* and *unbelievable* and *frightening*.

Now, though he can be surprisingly sensitive, Rod is a very down-to-earth fellow and not easily impressed. Up till then he had never seen a carp which had looked convincingly over the record. Now here he was, ranting like an inflamed vicar. And I believed every word of it.

"Things are looking good," he shouted over the final pips. "You'd be barmy not to come down."

Incredibly, I was doing some work then that I just couldn't drop on the spur of the moment and so it wasn't until the Friday, on a grey windy afternoon, that I arrived at the pool. The bankside trees were all bare, the surrounding fields looked bleak and cold. Compared with its summer appearance, Redmire seemed almost desolate.

I went to find Rod and discovered him, wet and bedraggled, still in

Ingham's Pitch. His canvas-draped brolly had not entirely protected him from the monsoon earlier in the week. He had no more fish to report since the twenty-two pounder, but he didn't think that carp was worth talking about. He was still wild with the thought of the giant. No one, he said, could ever begin to imagine the size of it. One had to see it for oneself.

"Jack Hilton reckons it's four feet long. I say it's bigger than that. It's as big as a man."

Despite the cool easterly wind I was brimming with confidence. First cast from the Willow Pitch produced a fourteen-pound common, as bright as an autumn beech-leaf. I'd not realised before just how a carp's colour intensified as winter approached. With the contrast of the leaden-grey water, my fish looked incandescent and I said it was a good omen. Rod, who hadn't had a touch for three days, said it was a sheer fluke.

Just before dark the clouds broke and cleared and the temperature began to plunge. A perfect excuse, we said, to spend the evening in the pub, discussing monsters.

Jack the Roadman was there, as usual, talking with his farmer friends about storm damage. He laughed when he heard that Rod had been fishing through the worst of the week's weather. "Yer storm-damaged yerself!" Mike and Sue, the only people in the pub of our own age, took pity on us. Frosts were forecast and they said we'd die of pneumonia without a good hot meal.

"Come to dinner at our cottage, tomorrow evening." Of course we accepted.

"We'll see you here for a drink first," I said.

"Seven o'clock then," said Mike.

October nights can seem interminable, especially when you remember the four-hour nights of midsummer. In autumn you wake from what you thought was a longish sleep and there is no sign of the dawn. You doze off, wake fully an hour later and still the sky is untinged with light. At least when the eastern horizon does begin to become obvious, the morning arrives quickly, almost with a rush – not like the gentle approach of a June day. Lying in my sleeping-bag, in the Willow Pitch, I spent an hour watching and then counting meteorites. But then cloud came over and the subsequent rise in temperature made me feel drowsy and I soon dropped off. A fox woke me at about 2 a.m. He'd come along the bankside path and discovered a sleeping man blocking his way. As he soundlessly picked his way round me I opened my eyes. The first thing I saw was an enormous dog-shaped silhouette against a dark grey sky. It didn't completely overwhelm me as I was still half-asleep. I couldn't understand it, though. It was too fantastic to be real, yet it obviously wasn't a dream. I wanted to frighten it away but discovered I could only move from the waist down. Was I paralysed? I made wild running motions inside my sleeping-bag and the fox let out a hoarse yelp and leapt into the air. When morning finally broke I blamed it all on last night's ale.

Bob Jones arrived at dawn and, before he set up his gear, he came round for a chat. Rod joined us and I put the kettle on. Rod had been stalking at the shallows, except there'd been nothing to stalk. Not a fish had stirred for hours, he said. Twenty yards out, though, I'd seen a stream of bubbles intermittently rising and, after two casts, had dropped a hookful of corn just to the left of their source. Now, as the kettle boiled, Bob said he was sure I was going to get a take. The bubble trail was moving left, becoming more persistent. It appeared so obvious that something was going to happen that I guessed we were going to be disappointed. In carp fishing there is very little that is inevitable. But then the line jerked and began to pour wonderfully off the spool.

"There you go!" said Rod, and both he and Bob moved back a yard as I leaned forward, closed the pick-up, and made contact.

For a moment I couldn't tell whether the fish was big or small. The rod was not severely bent, yet the carp was holding its ground. Then it began to rise, like a balloon coming free of its anchor rope, and we all peered into the water. It was deep and the fish seemed to take a long time to appear, but when it did we were struck by the brilliant colour. It was that autumn tint again, making the carp look like a giant goldfish, a burning contrast to the dark colourless water. It rolled lazily, then swung in an arc towards the treacherous willow stumps on our left. Bob hurried along the bank and, with a long branch, splashed the surface, causing the fish to veer suddenly. But it was moving quite slowly, almost casually, as if unaware of its predicament. In the meantime, Rod had donned waders and was now standing, ten feet out from the bank, net at the ready. The carp cruised past me, then past him and we both had a clear view of it: a solid-looking mirror, obviously over twenty pounds. I eased it to the surface and it woke up, lashing out with its tail and plunging away. Because of the lack of weed I was using light tackle – six-pound line and a number 10 hook – therefore I could not restrain a fairly determined run, straight out for nearly twenty-five yards. But when he turned I was able to keep him coming all the way to the net and we gave a little cheer

An autumn brace: Redmire carp of fourteen and twenty-four pounds.

as Rod gently heaved him up.

A portly, boldly coloured twenty-four pounder then sat for his portrait.

The day remained overcast and surprisingly mild. Bob discovered some fish feeding on the shallows and spent five hours trying patiently to outwit them, but they weren't interested in sweetcorn. But at least he had something positive to do; Rod and I spent the day watching unmoving reflections. At five o'clock, Bob packed up. Day-trips to Redmire were quite sensible if, like him, you lived only forty miles away. I took his parting advice and went to see if I could catch a fish on the shallows. But I couldn't even find one to cast at.

Just before sunset the sky cleared completely. The pool, which had been quite calm, gradually became intensely calm. The stillness would magnify any stirrings of feeding fish so I began to look around more hopefully.

I had an idea the Stile Pitch would be the place to try, but when I crept up to it I discovered Rod was already there. Sneaking past him, I went up to the islands. There was a large patch of bubbles rising only a few yards out from Bramble Isle but, on climbing a tree and looking down, I could see clearly the creature responsible: a large eel of perhaps four pounds, drilling into the mud for its supper.

I climbed to the top of the tree, scanned the entire pool, but the dark water looked devoid of life. There were no outward signs, yet I felt like a hawk who'd just spotted a rabbit in an open field. Suddenly I knew I was about to catch another big carp. I also knew *where* I would catch it, and before I could let reason begin its usual cold-water tactics (not that I ever listened to reason), I grabbed my rod and hurried round to the eastern corner of the dam – to the place where the old weed-filter jutted out from the brickwork. I baited a size 8 with two grains of corn and dropped it straight under the rod-tip, in about five feet of water. I was using a float, a yellow-tipped quill, and I scattered a small handful of corn around it.

I knew it must be about six o'clock, nearly time to start tidying ourselves up for our social evening. But I was appalled at the idea of leaving the water just when I'd sniffed out a possible monster. The blue sky was darkening, the float was beginning to merge with the reflections. The crescent moon turned from gold to silver.

Two bubbles rose to the surface. The quill lifted and began to slide away from me, but I was, for a moment, suspicious. I thought my eyes were being deceived by the twilight. I blinked. It was true; the float was definitely moving. Then it vanished completely and I made a gentle strike – just a quick lift of the rod-tip. Whatever was there went round in a tentative circle. I'd been expecting a tremendous resistance, but this felt like a sprat – until it decided that something was amiss. It pointed its head towards the centre of the pool and hurtled away.

Rod, hearing the long howl of the reel, came running up out of the gloom, net in hand.

"Stop playing around with it. If it goes any further it'll ground itself in the shallows."

He thought, at first, I was trying to impress him; allowing a small, quick fish to make a long run. But by the bend in the rod and my few stuttered words he soon realised I wasn't joking.

I've known carp make long dashes, even on quite heavy tackle, but that first flight, on six-pound line, was the longest single charge I've experienced. It was well over a hundred yards. To my horror, I suddenly realised I was being outrun. I'd lost almost all my line! Quickly I ran to the left, trying to lessen the angle and so gain some precious inches. The rod swung over, twisting in my grip, then began to fractionally unbend. It was like flying a kite and having it disappear over the top of a mountain – it seemed ridiculous for a hooked fish to have travelled so far.

Invisibly, the carp crashed on the surface and in the stillness the splash sounded like a man falling in headlong.

"As big as a man!" I thought, remembering Rod's description.

"It's a big one," I said.

Rod said something fairly blunt about my undeserved good luck, but he, too, seemed convinced I'd got into something large.

Incredibly, I seemed to be exerting some control, even though my tackle felt inadequate. I began to gain line quite quickly, in fact it seemed as if the fish was almost resigned to being towed all the way back to the dam. Then I noticed that the rod-tip was beginning to swing to the left, towards the old willow fifty yards away. Once under the sunken boughs the fish would say a snappy farewell and I yelled at Rod to go and throw something heavy. He dashed round, picked up the first thing he found (I think it was my camping stove) and hurled it into the pool. The pressure eased, my blood unfroze, the carp swung out into open water. I worked him almost under the rod-point, then he dived towards the Evening Pitch, over on the right-hand bank. After thirty yards I slowed and turned him and he gave a little wriggle and went solid.

There followed a few minutes of near nervous collapse. Rod tried to persuade me not to fall to pieces, but I thought it was all over, sure the line was inextricably snagged. Then the rod's fixed bend came alive again. It was as if the fish had become bored with lying still; after two or three minutes he just flicked his tail and glided majestically into deep water.

Because of my delicate tackle it was more of a balancing act than a fight. I had to feel carefully for those brief opportunities between dives, rolls and runs when the fish lost a little momentum and could be tilted this way or that and persuaded to yield a few yards before the next move. Parrying and cajoling, I eventually got him next to the dam wall. Then, gently but firmly, I tried to lift him from the bottom. Rod pushed the net into the water and flicked on a small torch. We saw the yellow-tipped quill float with a knot of weed-stems tangled round it. The float quivered just above the surface, but though I was straining the tackle to its limit the fish would rise only a foot or two in the water. Then it began to sink down again and we watched the quill slide back into the depths. There was another long-distance run, another slow haul back and then another attempt at a landing. I clenched my teeth and heaved and again the quill appeared, but only to rise about three feet above the surface. Rod shone the torch downwards and we peered into the murky depths – and gasped. There were the head and shoulders of a gigantic carp, hanging in mid-water, close to where Rod had sunk the landing-net. It loomed up for a moment and we stood transfixed. We had not imagined any carp could be so huge. But then Rod moved the net and the monster *unfolded*. We'd been looking at the wafting mesh, criss-crossed like the flank of a fully scaled carp. The dim torchlight had deceived us wonderfully.

It felt like a rod-wrenching, nerve-fraying eternity since I'd first hooked this fish and we seemed no nearer to landing it. The carp fought from a point near the centre of the dam, making continual runs, charges, and sudden turns and passes. To each move I was not much more than a spectator. The fish quietened occasionally, but when I enticed it back towards the net it refused to be raised. After a few moments, while it lurked on the bottom, recovering strength, it would turn and careen away again into deeper water. The stars were now shining brightly and the moon had curved quite a long way into the west. Amazingly, Rod never once mentioned the dinner we were meant to be eating. He was as convinced as I that this carp, whether it was the king or not, was an undoubted record-breaker. He was content to wait with the net all night if necessary and he kept reminding me to "take it easy".

It felt impossible to raise the fish within reach of the net and so the only alternative was to lead it into shallower water. There were shallows on the right-hand side of the dam, by the outfall, but I was anxious about the proximity of that rusty iron weed-filter, an ideal means of escape for a big wily carp. On the left-hand side the water was certainly shallow enough, but the hazards were worse. I began, therefore, to steer the fish towards the outfall and it responded in typical carp fashion, shooting off in the opposite direction. I raced after it, feeling (and hearing) the line pinging against the shrubs and brambles that trailed over the dam wall. Just before it reached the snag-infested corner, the carp made a surprise turn and dashed towards the Willow Pitch. Somehow, I brought him round and back in a wide arc and he began circling, just on the edge of the deeper water.

Though there were various submerged roots lying in wait for foolish anglers, the water under the rod-tip was only a yard deep. I reckoned that, with constant pressure and a large slice of luck, I could eventually bring the fish close enough to net. Rod, however, decided not to take any risks.

"I'm going in for it!" he declared, stripping off.

"What!" I gasped. "You'll freeze to death!"

The temperature had dropped at least twenty degrees since the afternoon and we could feel the frost in the air. But Rod was adamant. He would wade well out and net the fish as it came up out of the depths. He took off waders, socks and jeans and lowered himself off the dam wall.

"Ouch!" he said as he sank up to his waist in flesh-pincering water. He waddled forward and I brought the fish towards him; but still I couldn't raise it and I winced as it looked set on a collision course with Rod's legs. At the last moment it rocketed away and once more I warmed my cold fingers on a scorching spool.

Both my hands were completely numb by now and I was having to constantly change grip from right to left while I huffed and shook some life back into my fingers. I couldn't imagine what Rod was suffering, but as he clambered out and we followed the carp along the wall, he said not to worry, he was too cold to feel anything.

The fish had travelled three-quarters of the width of the pool, about seventy-five yards. Then it slowed and sulked and I wound my way past it until I stood near the point where we'd originally made contact. The weed-filter, looking like a half-submerged lion's cage, was next to me and Rod clambered precariously out onto the end of it. He lowered the net and I drew the monster towards us. It felt more ponderous now, less liable to explode in unexpected directions. I could imagine it dragging low over the lake bed leaving a long trail in the silt. It *had* to be huge. Earlier in the day, that twenty-four-pound mirror-carp had come to the net in five minutes, but here was a fish that had been charging like a war-horse after nearly *two hours*! And it was obvious, by the way it responded to pressure, that it wasn't foul-hooked.

Now, as the moon sank red to the horizon, it seemed as if the final moment had come. It rose to the surface and for the first time we saw broken water. There was a slow, lazy splash as it rolled and I wound down and leaned to the right, watching the black silhouette of Rod reach towards an equally black bow wave. The wave met the point where the net slanted into the water and my heart gave a little lift — and then plummeted into my boots. There was a tumultuous splash and the fish whirled round and surged away; just the touch of the net against his nose had been enough to drive him wild. And there was something terribly wrong. The line had somehow caught round the 'S' link that joined the net-cord to the arms so that the rod bent directly downwards while the carp rushed ten, twenty yards to my left. It seemed obvious that something would break.

I shouted out something unintelligible, but Rod knew what had happened and could even feel a vibration running down the net handle. He lifted the net sharply, shook it, and miraculously the line came free, though for a sickening moment it fell slack and I was convinced it had snapped. But then the tension swept back into the rod.

Reluctantly, the fish returned and this time Rod got him, smoothly lifting just as the carp wallowed between the net arms. But even then the drama wasn't quite over. There was a fierce eruption of water as it lashed out with its tail. Rod teetered and looked set to topple into the drink, but he steadied himself and waited until the storm had passed. Then he said, "Well, it isn't a record," and passed me the net handle. I heaved the carp up over the dam rail and instead of the anticipated half-hundredweight it felt almost disappointing. But of course I wasn't disappointed. It was an extraordinary fish, all the more so for *not* being a record-breaker. It had displayed more strength, cunning and endurance than any carp either of us had known, yet it was — for Redmire — only an average-sized fish.

The more we thought about it the more incredible it seemed that we had actually landed it — with the odds so heavily in its favour it *should* have escaped. We shone the torch on it as it lay in the mesh. Then it did look huge — but only in length. It was like a very big wild carp, almost a yard long and as solid and perfect as finely cast bronze. We noticed the large, rounded muscles at the base of the pectorals and remarked on the span of the tail. Truly a Hercules of the fishes. And though at twenty-four and a half pounds it is less than half the size of my largest carp, it remains my best.

We suddenly remembered our dinner date. Rod hurried off to change into something more comfortable and returned after a few minutes wearing an ex-army tank-suit. There was nothing else he had that was dry. I put the fish in a sack and lowered it carefully off the dam where it would remain until morning. Then still slightly dazed from the evening's drama, we drove to the Royal Arms. It was almost nine o'clock and everyone was wondering what had happened to us. Mike and Sue had just about given us up.

"You won't believe this," I said . . .

19
A CLASSIC OPENING

By the time I'd tied all my bags of gear, rods and camping equipment onto my rusted motorcycle it looked less like a machine and more like a two-wheeled sofa. Once it was moving, all the canvas and plastic bags billowed dangerously, and at 50 m.p.h. it felt ready to float into the air.

I wouldn't, by choice, have made the one hundred and fifty mile journey to Redmire by motorcycle. But a wheel had fallen off the car and it was 15th June – the day before the new season began. In 1973 it was our turn to enjoy the luxury of the first Redmire week.

Luckily, conditions were ideal for motorcycling – warm and windless – and I only fell off once. Riding down the last hill – the grassy slope above the pool – and singing like a drunk at an opera, I skidded sideways on a cow-pat and so reached the waterside in magnificent style. As I sorted out my wreckage, Rod came along the bank to greet me. His eyes were gleaming and he looked like a miser who'd been counting too much gold. He told me he'd just seen six of the biggest carp in England, all nose to nose under the weeping willow. No, the king was not amongst them, but Rod was convinced they were all over forty pounds.

Rod had been at Redmire for three days, using the time to observe and study the fish, watching their reactions to various baits and no doubt holding long, one-sided conversations with them. Bob Jones arrived at about six o'clock and we all sat down in the Evening Pitch, drinking tea and discussing prospects. Though I was burning with anticipation I said I wasn't happy about the phase of the moon. It was almost full and, as most anglers know, a bright moon could often spoil your chances of a fish. Rod just laughed. He said the carp had been feeding so voraciously the last few days, it would take more than a full moon to jade their appetites.

The sun sank over the edge of the valley and we began to prepare our tackle. Bob decided to pitch in the Fence, Rod was already installed in the Stile and I chose to fish the spot where I'd caught my first Redmire carp – a reedy, tussocky stretch of bank overhung with alders and willows, up near the shallows. The June twilight lingered almost to midnight and, waiting for that hour, I thought of all the possibilities of the coming season. Redmire was a wonderful place to be on the Sixteenth, all the more so when you were confident and justifiably optimistic – despite the moon.

Compared to my timorous approach to Redmire twelve months earlier I now felt like a lord. Call me precocious, but I was sure I'd mastered the place, that there could be no more insurmountable problems. This rather pompous attitude was brought about by comparing our first season's results with the rest of the syndicate's first-year catches. Only Rod and I had ever enjoyed such early success. Even Jack Hilton had only managed one twenty-pounder during his first full season.

Before we joined the syndicate Jack and Bill Quinlan were the only anglers who were regularly catching Redmire carp. There is no doubt that they were far more skilful than us, but what we lacked in skill we made up for in cranky inventiveness and unquenchable enthusiasm. The most important thing about our initial approach was that we had no fixed ideas. We weren't clogged up with established, traditional thinking, which was good because traditional methods didn't appear to work any more at Redmire. Really, we didn't know *what* we were doing, we simply made it up as we went along, from floating maggots to artificial moths, from mass-baiting with jelly babies to blow-piped sweetcorn.

Rod was much more original than me, always marching ahead with new ideas, novel baits, untried techniques and proposing theories that were often completely crazy. But he lacked my faith in the power of instinct.

In 1972 Redmire was still a poolful of mysteries, but Rod in particular and I in my small way had begun to solve those mysteries. And, of course, nowadays so much has been discovered that there are not many mysteries left to grapple with.

I noticed a glow radiating from behind me and turned to see the moon

A Classic Opening

rising over the fields. Down towards the dam a great fish walloped on the surface and the splash echoed into the night. Rising moon, leaping fish, the moments seeming to hang rather than pass, Redmire conjuring a rare atmosphere. It was enough to make you put your first cast into a tree.

A few seconds after midnight I dropped one bait well out into the centre of the pool and flicked a second, freelined, within a yard of a half-submerged tree, over to my left. I lay the rods flat on a groundsheet and was just arranging the foil indicators when there was a sound from the far bank exactly like the proverbial bull in the china shop. There were several heavy crashes and thumps and it was obvious that someone had put his foot in it. There followed a splintering, cracking noise, a grunt, the sharp *swish* of a rod and then the scream of a reel. Less than two minutes into the season and Rod had hooked a carp.

I listened appreciatively, enjoying this variation on a familiar theme. After a further sequence of odd noises, there was a short interval then a furious thrashing of water that stopped abruptly, though I could hear a fish still kicking, well wrapped up in the folds of a landing-net.

"How big?" I called, and after a minute the reply floated back.

"Twenty-two pounds. A leather."

Rod explained later that he'd been a few yards from the bankside when the fish picked up his bait. He'd leapt forward, completely forgetting his bait-cans, stove, cooking pots and tackle boxes. In the morning it looked as if an earthquake had happened in his pitch.

Half an hour after midnight it was Bob's turn. I heard him strike, heard his reel buzz. I ran down the bank and found him locked into a carp that had run well out into the pool and was still pulling strongly. But just as I picked up his landing-net I saw his rod jerk straight. The hook-hold had failed, though it was typical of Bob that he took the loss calmly and philosophically. Had it been me I would have raved about and chewed the ends off a few fence-posts.

The moon rose higher and began to glare. The air was now thin and very cold. The vast shadow of an elm was cast across me, hiding my presence, I hoped, from any night-patrolling carp. At about 2 a.m. I heard a quick stuttering hiss and swooped forward to see the foil on the left-hand rod sliding to the butt-ring. It stopped as I put my fingers on the reel-handle. For a moment I hesitated. But then, for no good reason, I struck and surprised myself by hooking a fish. The rod hauled over as something powerful rocketed under the half-sunken tree. Instantly I whipped the rod-tip into the water and leaned out as far as possible from the bank. The tackle was strong but nevertheless I winced when the carp rose up under the branches and flailed the surface. In the moonlight it looked as if a tremendous firework was going off. Sparkling droplets flew out of the black foliage and great outspreading waves glinted and flashed.

Hearing the explosion, Bob quickly arrived on the scene and a well-thrown clod drove the fish into open water. It made a magnificent circular sweep that arced directly back into its sanctuary. Bob sent in another clod and once more the fish lunged away. I was amazed not to have the line jam round a twig.

The carp slanted into deeper water and I began to be rather stern with it, not allowing it to get too far from me. While it was miraculous I hadn't lost it beneath the tree, there were many other sunken branches close by and I couldn't afford the luxury of a long line. With the rod actually creaking and the line chiming dangerously I brought my fish almost in range of the net. It turned over on the surface and we glimpsed a pale expanse of moonlit flank. Smashing the water with its tail it made a fierce turn, got its head down and arrowed far out into the pool. As soon as the reel stopped whining, I crammed on pressure, rolled the fish over and began pumping back, leaning hard to the left as it tried to swerve into the willow on our right. Bob missed once, then, waiting until it was completely between the arms, lifted smartly and in a moment a splendid twenty-five-pound mirror-carp was gleaming on the grass. The moon was reflected in every scale. So ended our opening night.

I was grateful that we should have the honour of first rights. We knew that Jack Hilton, arch-duke of Redmire, would be arriving in the morning and we guessed that our efforts would pale into insignificance once he began to exert his influence over the place. Such was Rod's sense of occasion — he'd had only one brief meeting with the great man before — that he became almost fastidious. The shambles of the Stile Pitch was transformed and within an hour it resembled an artillery position ready for the field marshal's inspection.

"I suppose you've even got a tie to match your waders," I snorted.

"Don't you think," he said, "that you should spruce your place up just a bit? Jack'd be horrified if he saw how we really fish. I mean, you haven't even got any rod-rests!"

"And your rods are held together with sticky tape," I said. "Not that that stops you catching carp."

By mid-morning Jack still hadn't arrived and so I thought I might

A Classic Opening

take Rod's advice and at least get my rods up out of the grass. After all, most modern carp-fishers possess efficient (and irritating) electrical bite-indicators, as well as custom-built rod-rests. Jack Hilton, while obviously not a complete stickler, was accustomed to seeing things done properly at Redmire, therefore it would be unwise to disquiet him with our casual, unorthodox approach and our old, weather-beaten tackle. Not possessing any rod-rests myself, I mounted my faithful sticks on a matched set of used milk bottles. Rod was visibly shaken when he came round to view the improvements. In fact he could hardly stand up for laughing.

At about mid-day, Jack's gleaming Jaguar coasted down the slope towards us. We went to greet him and the first thing he asked was whether we'd caught any carp. He was genuinely delighted when we described the incidents of our first night, though he commiserated with Bob on his loss.

"So, you're still getting them on corn then?" he said.

"Well," I said, "I am, but I don't know what Rod's using."

Rod went through the list of the baits he'd brought, all of them exotic and untried. The twenty-two pounder had taken a broad-bean, but he was now baiting with 'black-eyes' – or was it maples, or adukis or liquorice allsorts or caviare? Jack's eyes glinted as Rod told him about the monsters under the willow. He was convinced enough by the tale to decide there and then on his pitch and within a few minutes we were all helping him carry his gear round to Inghams.

The sky, which had been serenely blue all morning, suddenly darkened and a cool breeze sprang up from the west, blowing straight at me. I hadn't had a touch on corn since sunrise so it seemed wise to accept Rod's offer of a 'bag of lucky beans' and discover whether they'd work as instantly for me as they had for him. One bean was flicked under the willow on my right, the other cast next to the submerged tree on my left. I balanced the rods on their milk bottles, boiled a kettle, then sat back with a mug of tea to watch the swaying willows.

On the opposite bank I saw Rod dive forward and make a hurried strike. A huge wave began to bulge through the already rippling surface and it was obvious he'd hooked a corker. Jack, hearing the commotion of water and screech of reel, came running along the bank, net in hand. After a wild few minutes, Rod worked the fish nearer. It surfaced and even from my position, nearly a hundred yards away, it looked huge.

"It must be a good thirty!" Jack shouted.

But seconds later the hook popped out and Rod reacted in (our) time-honoured fashion: bellowing out a curse and hurling his rod like a javelin into the air. Despite the presence of the maestro he wasn't afraid of venting his emotions. It was a miracle he didn't throw Jack into the air as well.

An hour or so later a fish picked up one of my beans – the one on the left – and after a tussle, with Bob again being summoned for clod duty, I grassed a twelve-pound common. But the temperature was falling and the weather signs were not optimistic. We had no more carp that day and, in the deteriorating conditions, I had straight rods for almost a week. There was a cold, mean wind, leaden skies and torrential rain – ideal weather for sitting all day under a brolly, listening to the dribbling water, drinking tea and getting lost in a good book. Rod, the sly fox, crept round the pool every dawn before sunrise, while honest anglers were still asleep under the willows. He timed his rounds to coincide with the carp's brief feeding spells and after a couple of near misses he stalked and caught a fine twenty-four-pound mirror.

On the Monday Tom Mintram had arrived to take Bob's place, Bob having gone back to his school-teaching. Tom chose to fish the Willow Pitch but his lines hardly moved for three days. On the Wednesday afternoon, though, he had an experience that he will never forget, though I rather think Tom would like to. He heard a gigantic splash off the dam, over to his right. It had to be a colossal fish to make such a commotion, in fact Tom said it sounded like a cow falling in. A few moments later the line on his right-hand rod began to run out and, glancing out from under his brolly (it was still pouring with rain), he saw that a cow *had* fallen in. It must have leant too heavily on the dam rail as it craned over for a drink and – crack, splosh! After swimming across the corner of the pool and through Tom's lines it managed to scramble out and rejoin the herd.

When Rod heard this story he said he was sure Tom was telling a fib. He accused him of deliberately baiting with a blade of grass and tempting the cow into his swim, there being nothing else to fish for. He wrote his version of events down in the form of an epic poem which he then read out as Jack, Tom and I fell about laughing. Tom nearly swallowed his pipe.

If I was nonplussed about the straightness of my own rods, both Rod and I were impressed with the straightness of Jack's. The fact that only one of them had bent in four days, and then only briefly, convinced us that he wasn't a god after all. It must be said, though, that – complaining of overwork – Jack had spent most of his time in his bivouac, asleep.

A Classic Opening

And when he did emerge his fishing was hardly intensive. Conditions being poor, he was more interested in exchanging fishing stories with his old friend Tom.

I suppose there comes a stage in every successful angler's life when he feels his appetite for big fish becoming jaded. And so, as there were times in his early days when the urge to fish was irresistible, there are also times in later years – especially after four cold, wet days at the waterside – when there is an equally irresistible urge to go home. It was blasé of Jack, though, to pack up on the very day the fish began to move. Perhaps it was something to do with Rod and me. Jack probably knew we would soon be leaping along the banks like children chasing grasshoppers. He left poor Tom to endure our wild exuberance.

And Jack's reaction to my antique tackle and Rod's anarchic attitude? Well, I don't know exactly what he said to Rod, but he was certainly interested in his new ideas and not at all sceptical. However, while he might have raised an eyebrow at the battered state of Rod's tackle, he was obviously dubious about some of my old rods and reels. My rod-rests understandably perplexed him. One day, as we sat on the dam, Jack enjoying a cigar and me trying to tempt a carp on float-fished corn, using a floppy cane rod and a gritty centre-pin reel, he asked, "What would happen if you hooked a really good fish on that gear?" I replied that it would be the same as when I hooked an averagely good fish, except the excitement might last longer. (It was ironic that the very next time we met I was just returning a thirty-eight-pound mirror-carp, caught from that precise same spot on the dam, using the same tackle. I even used the same porcupine-quill float!)

For four days I'd seen not a sign of carp or even sensed their presence. The pool wore a completely blank expression, like the face of a genius who had suddenly run out of ideas. And then, in the space of a few hours, the air, that had been thin and cold, became soft and mild, heavy with the scents that were unique to Redmire. The atmosphere visibly thickened, hazing the distant hills, mellowing the colours of the landscape. The pool came to life again, its dark surface becoming an alphabet of V's and O's as carp bow-waved this way and that or leapt and sent the ripples wheeling.

A warm breeze sprang up, blowing down towards the south-east corner of the dam. Rod, the carp hound, followed it, found a group of big carp browsing in the shallow, weedy water and quickly fetched his tackle. Tossing in a few handfuls of beans he soon had the fish nosing down enthusiastically. After half an hour, just as I was creeping down the bank towards him, he leapt into action. He struck and an obviously large carp whirled round, making a dark hole in the water and sending up a shower of spray. It bow-waved through a dense weed bed and soon clamped itself firmly in the aquagrowth. Winding as he went, Rod plunged straight in. I followed behind with the net and together we waded to within a few yards of the fish. As Rod held firm, I edged forward, pushing the net under when I reached a sort of knot in the weed stems. The carp dashed suddenly away, sending up another shower of spray and flinging bits of weed into my face. "Mind the line!" shouted Rod, as the fish swerved cunningly round. I ducked and waddled out of the way, and Rod continued his pursuit.

Luckily, the carp never managed to get out of the shallow corner of the pool. The weed was so thick that, had the fish gained the deeps, Rod may not have been able to unclog it. Finally, he eased it to the surface where it lay quite still, cocooned in weed stems, while I slid the net under it. A quick lift, a churning splash and Rod chalked up his third twenty-pounder of the week.

In the evening the breeze died down and the carp began to move up the pool. I watched them drifting past me, just vague grey shapes creasing the inverted sunset. Taking a rod and some bait I followed them all the way up to the inlet stream where, in the shallow weed-free water, they began to feed. I embedded a number 6 hook neatly in a single broad bean and, with nothing else to weight the line, made a slow, floating cast that dropped the bait amongst the fish as gently as a leaf. Then I made myself comfortable, half-hidden by a willow branch. The carp were making the shallows bulge and ripple as they rooted through the silt for their favourite delicacy – bloodworms. What must a great broad bean look like to a fish who is only interested in microscopic food? Surely carp would regard such an offering with suspicion, if not contempt? I scattered a few broken-up bits of bean across the water and hoped the fish might fancy some vegetables with their meat.

It was a perfect midsummer eve; the western sky smouldering with hot colour, the air warm and fragrant, the birdsong clear, the pool rich in promise. The moment was enough in itself and it seemed wrong to ask for anything more – even at Redmire; but then something moved and, almost jarringly, snatched me out of my dream. The line was cutting a little V through the surface film and before it was properly tight I struck and sent a carp ploughing down the pool. It went only about ten yards, then I rolled it over and, being as firm and yet as careful as possible, brought it zig-zagging into the net. The first fish in days was a bright, deep-bodied ten-pounder. There were others three times his size still browsing, seemingly unconcerned, so I quietly released him and re-cast. Within minutes I'd landed another but it was smaller, not bigger, than the first — a common of about six pounds.

The second disturbance was too much for the other fish though they didn't melt completely away; they shifted their ground until they were just out of my casting range. I waited patiently for over an hour, as the light sank into the west and the bats and moths replaced the swifts and swallows. Then again my line spilled off the reel and this time I hooked something that wouldn't be checked. A long, straight wave, reflecting the blue of the afterglow, pencilled across the dark pool. It disappeared suddenly under the silhouette of a willow and the next moment I saw the water creaming. Rod and Tom, chatting down at the far end of the lake, both heard the long howl of a reel followed by a big splash. Rod made a long-distance run and arrived on the scene just as I began to gain a few yards of line. Somehow, I managed to keep the carp on the move, piloting it through the worst of the snags until Rod could reach it with the net.

It was a beautiful fish, in fact one of the loveliest carp I've ever seen; elegant, streamlined, dark as jet. The outline of the scales reflected the twilight so that it seemed shrouded in silver mesh. The weight was just over seventeen pounds.

I moved back to my original pitch for the night, thinking it worthwhile to sit with a rod until dawn. I put a bait in the "hot-spot"; just off the edge of the submerged tree. Once I'd settled down to wait, though, I realised that the carp — in fact the whole landscape, the whole world — seemed to be sinking into a profound sleep. The air remained mild and still and the night was intensely quiet; not a ripple or a splash, not an owl-moan, rat-rustle or distant road-drone; I couldn't even hear the faint whisper of the overspill. Though there were no sounds of fish movement there was an undeniable *smell* of carp. It was the first time I'd consciously sensed carp en masse, through my nose! (In later summers I learnt to associate that particular smell with the carp's spawning

Seventeen-and-a-half pounds of fishy perfection.

time and presume there must be a fishy equivalent to musk.)

Despite the utter stillness I wasn't tempted to slide under a blanket and join everything else in sleep. I was tired but also expectant, thinking this great calm was somehow portentous – the lull before the storm.

The half-moon appeared at around 3 a.m., rising up out of a pale haze that was the first touch of the new day. And soon after, the silver foil signalled a bite, though it only moved a few inches then hung quivering between ground and rod. Nothing further happened and eventually I reeled in and found that not only had the bait gone from the hook, the hook had gone from the line. The shank had been bitten clean through leaving me with just the eye! I tied on another one, re-baited and re-cast.

The stars faded into the dawn sky. On the west bank the trees lost their dark outlines and began to fill with dimly lit foliage. A mist began to slide across the surface. It was now about an hour from sunrise and still nothing had broken the silence – not a carp-leap or cock-crow.

Perhaps, as had happened before, the carp would return to the shallows for an early breakfast. But when I looked, there was nothing. I crept back to my pitch and sat down by the rod just as the silver foil rose smoothly to the butt-ring. I struck, and before the reel even clicked the rod was wrenched almost out of my hands. Such savage power seemed overwhelming, especially after the hours of deep calm. I let the pull drag me to my feet and then the reel sang out. Something swooped under the tree and,

A Classic Opening

repeating the tactics of the twenty-pounder, rocketed up into the half-submerged branches. The dawn shook with a thunderous splash. It sounded more than loud, it was supernatural. No carp, however big, could make such a noise.

I pushed the rod deep underwater and prayed for the line to hold. It was ten-pound breaking-strain, and new, yet it felt as fragile as button-thread as it jagged through the clawing twigs. There was another great splash; the rod shuddered and creaked. I jumped in, thinking to get a better angle of pull if I waded out level with the fish. When I was about waist-deep the carp suddenly reacted to the changing pressure, surging into the open lake. Trying to stop it was like trying to halt an avalanche. There was a deep ponderousness about it, completely different from the pull of all the previous fish. The rod pulsed in its curve and I was sure I could feel the sensation of a large, rhythmically swaying tail, driving the carp forward.

Where were Rod and Tom? Surely this localised thunderstorm had shaken them out of their sleeping bags? I shouted and whistled, hoping for someone to come and at least pass me the net. But no one answered. I couldn't believe it! Did they need a bomb to wake them?

The whole upper half of the pool was furrowed with great ripples and once, when the fish turned and charged into the shallows, a wave went by at least a foot high. Some fifteen minutes passed then, just after I'd coaxed the fish out of the willows on my right, it surfaced quite close to me. I saw a pale grey flank and an enormously wide tail that slapped down, creating a small whirlpool as it thrust away. There was at least one more visit to the submerged tree and another epic journey towards the dam before I began to even think about the net. Then, waiting until things were reasonably calm, I waded clumsily backwards, grabbed the net, propped it under my arm and tried to persuade the fish to come in. It wouldn't. It boiled on the surface, threw up a fountain and slowly chugged off to the far bank. I watched a bow wave disappear into the mist and it was a while before it reappeared.

At least four times I brought the carp almost to the net, only to have it veer off at the final moment. I began to get desperate, lunging forward and trying to wade to the fish – always a fatal mistake in open water. Twice I stumbled and nearly went under. But then the resistance ebbed and the carp floated over the mesh.

Twenty-nine and three-quarter pounds it weighed, which was less than I'd expected. It was very large in frame, but rather hollow; an ancient,

grey-flanked, almost prehistoric-looking mirror-carp. It possessed the widest tail span of any fish I've ever caught; seventeen inches across.

A gold sun rose into a clear sky. I lay down under the willows to be lulled asleep by a gently cooing wood-pigeon. After five hours I woke feeling a bit groggy. The day had become very hot and sultry and my head was buzzing like a bee-hive. I wandered round the pool to see how Rod and Tom were getting on. They too complained about the heat and said the fish were only interested in basking.

Rod and I went scouting round the top of the pool. We climbed into a willow and, from the upper branches, watched the dark form of a carp cruising over the sunstruck shallows. One or two other fish came slowly into view, not swimming aimlessly, but moving dead-ahead as if on a fixed course. We recognised that purposefulness. For the first time in a week the carp were going to feed on the shallows in the afternoon.

Rod and Tom moved up to the old withy beds, on the west bank; I went back to the last gap in the willows by the feeder stream, on the east bank. As we cast, the fish were already beginning to stir up the first clouds of red mud. I didn't have to wait long before I saw a slight furl of water spread out from where my bait was lying. I was holding the

A Classic Opening

rod with the reel pick-up closed and all I needed to do as the line tightened was gently flick my wrist.

There was a plunging splash, as if someone had tossed a boulder in, and then a bow wave went streaking down the pool. It disappeared from sight as it went round a group of leaning willow trees. The two anglers opposite looked on bemused, though they had to admit to being impressed by the bend in my rod. They had a clear view of the carp's line of flight and watched it break surface at the end of its run and perform a complete backward somersault. That tremendous rush – almost seventy yards – seemed to have taken the steam out of it. I pumped it back fairly easily and it was soon churning the water in front of me. Holding it on a shortish line I waited for Rod to come round with the net.

"How big is it?" he asked as he peered into the muddied pool.

"I think it's *quite* big." I replied. "Perhaps another twenty-pounder."

The carp made a lunge for a single, sunken willow branch and rather too easily wrapped the line round it, bringing proceedings to an abrupt halt.

"Twenty pounds?" cried Rod, as the fish lay, clearly visible on the surface. "I doubt if it'll go twelve!"

I couldn't believe it. The initial run had all the power of a runaway horse, and I was using strong tackle, yet I had to agree – the fish didn't look big at all.

It wouldn't shift and Rod wasn't going in for it. At least not to begin with. Then he said, "Oh hell! It's a nice day for a dip." So he stripped off and began wading through the thick, glutinous mud. Before he was waist deep, the carp somehow detached itself from the snag, though not from the line. It didn't like the menacing sight of Rod's knees and I had a dreadful job bringing it in. It would have been easier if Rod had waded ashore, but he was enjoying himself too much, wallowing in the glorious mud and pulling faces at the fish. Over on the far bank, old Tom sadly shook his head.

Either this was a miraculously strong twelve-pounder or we needed our eyes tested. When we finally got it in the net we found the latter to be true. It *was* a twenty-pounder. A twenty-one-pound male common, perfectly proportioned, in flawless condition.

This experience intrigued us as our judgement of the size of fish in water had usually been quite accurate. But later incidents showed that we nearly always underestimated the weight of a big carp on the shallows, while those we saw and caught in deep water were usually weight-guessed

A twenty-one-pounder from the Redmire shallows.

correctly. You'd think it would be the other way around.

All afternoon and early evening big carp paraded up and down the shallows, some singly, some in groups. A trio of very large mirrors nosed down for a scattering of beans as I watched from the branches of a tree. The upper lobes of their tails waved in the air as they vacuumed every scrap of food off the bottom. I was able to climb down and pick up my rod with the fish grubbing about virtually at my feet. It was a simple matter to drop a bean straight under the nose of the biggest one and I was convinced he would snaffle it without hesitation. But I suddenly decided, to my surprise, not to cast. I was content; I'd had my fill of the cream.

The fish were so close to me and I could see them so clearly that it was a pleasure to simply lean back against the tree and watch them peacefully browsing.

Before sunset I decided the only thing I wanted to do was sleep. In any case, all activity in the pool had ceased and Redmire lay still and silent in the evening light. I'd been asleep for about three or four hours when I was startled awake by what I thought was a herd of cattle stampeding through the margins. The uproar was so abrupt and terrific that I had a moment of quite sharp fear. It wasn't cattle. The carp had started to spawn.

Though it was too dark to see anything but dim clouds of spray, it was obvious that more and more fish were hurling themselves into the annual frenzied ritual, and the tumult seemed to be centred a few yards in front of my pitch. From sounding like a stampede of cattle the noise generated into something akin to a volcanic eruption. The party went on all night and I was mad not to have crawled off to sleep in a distant field or a barn. By the time it was over I felt like a man suffering from shell-shock.

I've witnessed many carp spawnings at different lakes and also other spawnings at Redmire, but I have never experienced anything like that furious night of June 1973.

On that resounding note our eventful week drew to a close – well, at least it had been eventful for Rod and me. It was unfair, though, that we'd caught all the carp while Tom had only caught a cow.

Redmire

PART IV

Carps and Beer
INCIDENTS CONCERNING THE GOLDEN SCALE CLUB

Hops and turkeys, carps and beer
Came into England all in a year.

From The Chronicle of Sir Richard Baker (1530

He delights in big floats and big baits, but not in strong
tackle; he prefers his tackle to be of ripe age. He used
to treasure a greenheart spinning-rod that, like a Bactrian
camel, had two humps. The least grilse or pickerel, you
would have thought, might be the straw to break its back.
Scott cherished it with a fearful love.

C. V. HANCOCK *Rod in Hand* (1958)

The Golden Scale Club was never officially founded, nor does it appear on any register of angling clubs. It has resisted affiliation, organisation, politicisation, complication, and a man called Boris who lives in Farnham, Surrey.

The club was formed like flotsam; various oddments came together by chance. The members have in common a fondness for vintage fishing tackle, overgrown carp ponds and musty old pubs. They share, too, a dislike for the way many of today's angling attitudes reflect the urgency, competitiveness and cheerlessness of modern times. In fact it could be said that the G.S.C. is a reaction to those attitudes.

As the vice-chairman put it: "The trouble with angling nowadays is that it's become too serious."

20

THE FIRST FOUR DAYS

15TH JUNE: The Golden Scale Club called at my cottage* for me on their way to the opening-night venue. We were going to fish a forest pond on the Surrey borders and, as the club members sat down for tea and I bundled some rods and tackle together, we agreed that so long as there was a chance of a carp each we'd be content. All we hoped for was that the pond would be reasonably quiet so that the true carp-fishing atmosphere would get a chance to brew before midnight. That atmosphere was all-important, for without the right feeling to the fishing there was no point in it.

As we set off in convoy through the winding lanes to the fishery, I remembered that it was two or three years since we'd last been there, so I was half-prepared for the shock when we finally arrived. The pond was almost sold out. There was hardly a pitch vacant, except for a boggy stretch of bank up in the shallows. "Another population explosion!" said Dandy, our chairman.

We decided to make the best of it. At least we would fish together, well away from the massed rod emplacements that looked like shore batteries preparing to repel the German navy. After we'd set up (all with cane rods and a wonderful lack of electrical devices) we went round to a nice old pub I knew, only a mile distant, where we could wash away our initial disappointment.

Leaning against the bar, we began to recover lost optimism. A discussion began on the qualities that go to make the classic opening; then someone began to recite, by heart, a passage from "B.B.'s" *Confessions of a Carpfisher* and our memories went back to the tranquil evenings of years gone by. Someone else produced a battered volume of 1930 fishing stories and proceeded to read out an evocative description of the perfect carp pool. By closing time, all but one of us was keen to get back for the 'off'.

"It's no good," said Main Beam, the club idealist. "I can't go back there. I'm going off to find some *real* carp fishing." He jumped on his motorbike and rode off into the night. Of course, we all knew how he felt, but it was too late to start wandering down dark lanes, searching for some carp pool of the past.

*In 1978 I bought a cottage in a wood on the Hampshire/Surrey border.

We got back to the pond, hoping that darkness would obscure the presence of the hordes of deadly earnest carp anglers. But we needed more than darkness: we needed earplugs as well. All round us was a noise like a giant computer suffering from violent indigestion. The bristling clusters of buzzers were being tested for faults. I dived into my sleeping-bag – head first.

16TH JUNE: Opening night was like a war against an invisible army as the massed ranks on the shore sent their baits and leads hurtling towards the skulking fish. It was easy to imagine the situation from the carp's point of view. After months of sublime peace, half a ton of bait and hardware suddenly drops out of the blue, and even a particularly dim carp is not exactly going to be fooled by such an unsubtle approach.

By sunrise, only one fish had been caught – and this was an easy, 'hungry' water. Before 6 a.m. we'd had enough and went trooping back to the peace and quiet of my home for an early breakfast. We felt like soldiers on leave from the trenches. "Christ!" said Anglepen, the archivist, "I knew we weren't likely to have the pool to ourselves, but that was incredible!" After something to eat and a few mugs of tea, the other members decided that Main Beam had had the right idea after all. They decided to go in search of more harmonious surroundings. A glutton for punishment, I said I was going back for another bash at the forest pond. I wasn't going to be outdone by an "easy" water. I'd meet the rest of the club the next day, down in Sussex. So we parted company: the Golden Scale Club went south, hoping to sample some vintage carp atmosphere; I gritted my teeth and returned to the forest.

Stalking would do the trick, I thought, as I looked in some reed beds and found signs of feeding fish. I crept along the spongey margins and lowered a single chick-pea next to a quivering reed stem. Within seconds, the line tightened and I struck. The rod went over, but kept curving more and more as the fish dived towards me, getting well into the tangle of underwater roots. A friend of mine, Barry Timms, was fishing nearby and he came up with his net to lend a hand. He waded into the reeds and the fish bolted, then thrashed on the surface as the snagged line checked its rush. Barry began to laugh. "It's a tench!" he said. The tench got its head down, bolted and broke me. Barry staggered about in the water, having hysterics. "Call yourself a carp-fisher," he said. "You can't even catch a tench!" He went off, chuckling, and I tied on a new hook, more determined than ever to get a carp.

I soon found another twitching reed stem and watched as a carpy-looking patch of bubbles rose next to it. Once more I lowered a bait into the murky depths. The line tightened and I struck. Barry came trotting back as he heard the splash and saw the rod go over. I got the fish into his net and he began roaring with laughter again. It was another tench.

"At least I put him on the bank," I said.

"Yes," laughed Barry. "All two pounds of him!"

I gave up after that and went home for tea. To add insult to injury, Barry came with me and ate nearly all the chocolate cake that some nice person had just taken out of the oven.

17TH JUNE: At 5 a.m., a poor imitation of an owl-call signified the arrival of Rick Birtwhistle Ford, president of the club. He hadn't been able to make the opening night (lucky fellow) having just got back from a two-day 'event' in Somerset. I leaned out of my window to see him swinging on the garden gate. "Good party, was it?" I asked.

We had some breakfast, then went over to a large lake not far from home to see whether it was worth fishing. (We'd arranged to meet up with the rest of the club at sunset, so had all day before we needed to set off for Sussex.) Some big carp were cruising in a reedy bay, but two anglers were already installed there. We went to see how they were doing.

"Any sport?"

"No."

"Anyone else caught anything?"

"No."

"Ever caught anything here before?"

"No."

"Ever seen anything caught?"

"No."

"Pickled fudge?"

We wandered off round the lake and spent the rest of the morning watching fish, letting the sight of them fire our enthusiasm for the coming night. At six we set off down the winding lanes (we always use the winding lanes when going carp fishing; never the smelly main roads). I was on my 900 cc motorbike, Birti was doing his best to keep up in his Citroen. By some freak of misjudgement, we got lost.

The rest of the club waited a while at the pre-arranged meeting place then went on to the chosen lake without us. By the time we'd zig-zagged a few times across the country and found them, it was nearly dark. Actually, we didn't find them, only their cars. We were just parking next to them when two bailiffs confronted us. "Are you syndicate members?" they asked. "What syndicate?" we asked, sweetly.

There was to be no fishing for us at that pool, though I wondered how the others had managed to get on the water. Either they'd avoided the bailiffs, or fooled them. Luckily, I remembered a lovely little wildie pool only ten miles distant, so we headed for it, hoping that it hadn't been turned into a match lake.

We arrived at the ancient farmhouse just as the farmer was thinking of bed. He was a friendly old soul, though, and after saying that we could certainly fish his pool, he even showed us the way through the dark yard and down a newly made path through the trees to the waterside. It was a relief to find that nothing had changed in all the years since we'd last fished there. We sat by the silent pool, ringed in by trees and the new night, knowing we were the only anglers there. We saw ripples circling the starlit water. This was the real carp fishing; alone with the clicking of the bats, the owl's hoot and the sucking of the carp in the lilies.

18TH JUNE: Nothing came to our rods that night, but as the first light of the new day touched the sky there was a great shout from Birtwhistle. I went running along the bank to find him crouched by a lily bed, his rod nicely curved and a good fish wallowing on the surface. After a tight struggle, we got him in – a superb wildie, just over eight pounds. He looked like a bar of gold left out in a shower of rain.

As the light increased I wandered round the pool, looking for feeding fish. There were bubblers, but I didn't manage to tempt one.

It seemed a whole day had passed by lunch-time – seven hours of daylight gone, yet another nine to go. The farmer came down for a chat and, seeing us wondering at the identity of a large hawk, suggested it might be "one of those grey hawks with long legs that stands very still".

The First Four Days

But if he wasn't an ornithologist he was an authority on the local pubs. We went to one of his favourites and were well rewarded by the quality of the beer and food, served in a quiet bar that overlooked a deep, wooded valley.

When we got back to the pool, I found the sun had brought the carp up to bask in the weed beds. I put out a crust, not far beyond a very long-looking fish, then inched it back until it was just over his nose. He took it with hardly a second glance. The line drew taut and I struck and *missed*. Five minutes later I had another perfect chance – but again I missed it. Third time lucky, and a slow, gurgling suck was soon followed by a great splash as the water broke and up shot a glistening bronze form, firmly attached to my line. It dived into the weed and fought pretty well, considering it was only half the size of Birti's fish.

Afternoon gradually became evening. We were joined by a small (and surprisingly quiet) crowd of village boys who, I suppose, must always descend on the pond as soon as school is over. By sunset, they were all gone again and we were left in peace with the carp.

I set up a pitch by the ancient oak sluice, where the water dribbled away into the wood below the dam. Two bottom baits were cast twenty-five yards out, in deep water, close to a large bed of weed. The trickle from the sluice lulled me towards sleep and I thought about the seventeen-pounder that had been caught a few years earlier. I tried to imagine what a true wild carp of that size would look like and ended up dreaming about it.

19TH JUNE: Dawn began to wash away the stars and a luminous mist floated across the pool's surface. In the early chill I wished I'd packed my tea-making gear. As usual, I'd brought only the bare essentials of tackle but, at that moment, I would have swapped one of my cane rods for a steaming mug of tea. I hadn't even brought any food, apart from a loaf of bread which was meant for the carp and I'd already eaten most of that.

Birtwhistle came round with the remains of his provisions: one orange. He generously halved it and we sat on the oak sluice gate, eating our meagre breakfast and complaining at the lack of activity.

"What I'd like to hear now," I said, "is the steady hiss of a running line." In a few minutes it happened and the rod-tip quivered as the line went streaming through the rings. I set the hook and a wave bulged into the weed beds. The small, floating leaves suddenly bunched together, like an anemone, as the fish dived. The clutch sang out, the rod lunged forward. For a while it stuck, solid and stubborn, in the weed stems, but then came that satisfying easing of pressure and the fish began to come clear. My heart lifted as we saw the line cutting through open water. Birti got the net ready and in a few minutes the carp was hammocked in the mesh. Another eight-pounder. It glowed in the first beams of sunlight.

We fished on for a few more hours, then Birti had a bright idea. His in-laws lived at a lakeside cottage about twelve miles distant and he was confident that a good breakfast could be found there. So we packed up, said goodbye to the farmer after paying him for the fishing ("Sorry lads," he said, "it's four bob a day now") and set off for much needed sustenance.

"Of course you're welcome to breakfast," said Birtwhistle's mother-in-law, "but first you've got to catch those three ferocious pike in my garden pond. They're eating the pet crucians!" Apparently, the pike had got into the pool via a feeder stream from the nearby lake. It didn't take us long to find them, skulking under lily pads and bunches of iris. With breakfast as the prize, we set to work like a couple of Fred Bullers and in ten minutes we'd hooked all three fish – and lost them! They'd bitten through the lines. Birti found a couple of rusty traces in his bag and we were soon back to the fray, baiting with greater pond snails and dropping the dainty morsels right on the shovel faces of the still-visible pike. They must have been as starving as we were and we soon had the pond churned

"It glowed in the first beams of sunlight."

to foam as the little sharks again cartwheeled across the water. We took each one back to the main lake, then strode into the cottage kitchen demanding our reward.

We set on our breakfast like a couple of jackals. I apologised between mouthfuls for not being the perfect guest, but survival comes before etiquette. Birtwhistle, whose appetite is famous (even when he's not hungry), said nothing. Thus fortified, we rode off again into the bright June morning. Birti had been reminded that it was his wedding anniversary and thought he'd better go home and celebrate. I headed for the Kent border. Rod Hutchinson was fishing at some desolate pit and I wanted to see how he was getting on with a certain monster mirror-carp. What happened next is his story, not mine.

21

FAR FROM THE MADDING CROWD

For years, we used to lease a pretty, overgrown carp lake on a farm in mid-Sussex, but in 1978 we had to give it up when the farm changed hands and the new owner proved to be rather unsporting.* During those years, with the club wallowing in tranquil seclusion and me spending most of my summers (except those of 1974–76) at Redmire, something was happening at all the other peaceful carp waters we used to fish. They were being invaded. A new army of carp-anglers had formed itself, vast and superbly equipped; its one aim was to put huge quantities of carp on the bank as efficiently and unemotionally as possible.

---

*A few years later the farm changed hands again and the new owners, generous folk, were happy to let us return to the lake.

We had been confronted by this army's vanguard earlier in the decade, on our occasional visits to the chain of lakes and pits along the Darenth Valley, in Kent, but by 1979 it seemed to have advanced right across the south of England. Walking round some of the places we used to know, we found the carp-anglers slotted like rows of cabbages along well-tended banks. Their tailor-made pitches were bristling with flashy, lethal-looking equipment and they wore fixed expressions of steely resolve, as if they were contemplating murder. The uniformity, the mechanical style of fishing and the slightly brittle atmosphere reminded me more of match fishing than carp fishing.

It seemed that, to a large degree, carp fishing had not only lost some of its essential spirit, it had also lost its point.

Of course it wasn't always so dismal and there were, in fact, times when a seething bank of crack carp-fishers provided a welcome opportunity for serious anarchy – like holding casting competitions in the middle of the night, or conducting midsummer carol concerts or fishing from bicycles. But it wasn't exactly traditional carp angling and, whatever happened, we were determined never again to open the season in the blitz conditions described in the previous story. Once more, we began to look for some remote, sequestered pond or lake where we might recapture the old magic.

Someone told me of the lakes along the valley of the little River Lod and, late one August, I went off to explore. Firstly, I came to a picturesque, reed-fringed mill pond, but another club had the lease. I followed the course of the river for a mile or two then found my way barred by a sidestream. The stream ran down out of a tunnel of dense, overhanging greenery and I could hear the sound of falling water. I pushed under the foliage to investigate and caught sight of a flickering, like a white flame, through the leaves. It was the spray cascading from a high, stone-faced outfall. I climbed up one side of it and found myself on a tree-hung dam. And there was Rivertree, stretching away in front of me, shining in the afternoon sun.

There was a rickety landing-stage jutting out from the dam and I stepped onto it to properly view the scene. It was a good-sized lake, perhaps five acres, surrounded by tall trees and thick hedges. On the southern bank, half hidden by elder bushes, was an ancient stone barn with a row of pigeons sitting on its roof. All the signs were good; no shaven undergrowth, no bare earth showing along the banks, no hook packets or beer cans. There were a number of landing-stages but they all looked ready

Where could we recapture the old magic?

to collapse and become driftwood. Several large trees had toppled full length into the water and now looked like the petrified bones of amphibious dinosaurs. It's a sight I love to see at a carp pool, firstly because the decaying branches are as much a roost for the fish as they are for the herons and kingfishers, and secondly, because great waterlogged trees give a lake an historic, almost haunted atmosphere.

The water was intensely calm, the tree-lined banks perfectly mirrored on the surface. In the entire scene, nothing had moved or made a sound for all the time I'd been watching. But then, not twenty yards out, a fish rose vertically into the air, appearing and then disappearing in a magical kind of slow motion and causing just a whisper of a splash. It was as if I'd imagined it, but the ripples were still wheeling out and I was sure

I hadn't mistaken the long, clean shape of a wild carp. A dog barked, over at the left-hand corner of the lake, and I suddenly noticed a house there. It nestled so snugly amongst the trees that it was easy to overlook, especially if your eyes had been stolen by the lake. I wandered over to it, vaguely anticipating a friendly meeting: it didn't look the sort of place where you'd be seen off by a mastiff or a shotgun. I found the owner and, sure enough, he was a pleasant, good-hearted farmer, but one who – it turned out – knew all about the perils of leasing waters to angling clubs.

"Nothing but a load of trouble in the end," he said. "They kept organising matches and, oh, what a performance!"

I tried to convince him that there were other kinds of anglers – men who desired peace and quiet in unspoilt surroundings as well as a good catch of fish. He listened to me patiently, with a half-smile on his lips that looked like the beginnings of an apologetic refusal. But he didn't refuse me. I made no special offers, simply promised to show respect towards his lake and his farm; and he said the Golden Scale Club would be welcome to fish, for a very reasonable charge, whenever we liked.

What had won him over, I think, was my description of the club as a bunch of harmless eccentrics, for he was bit of an eccentric himself.

Rivertree was a wonderful lake to have found and I felt the same kind of euphoria over its discovery as I had, nearly twenty years earlier, when I stumbled on the Island Pond and the Haunted Pool. It was the ideal Golden Scale Club water, having all the classical attributes: it was centuries old and, at one period of its history, it had been a monastery stew-pond. The fish were the true, old-English wildies and only the most ancient of the present bankside oaks had been standing when the first carp went in. The farmhouse was built on the remains of the monastery, which had been moated. Two shallow overgrown channels were all that was left of the moat which, unfortunately, had been filled in some years ago. The lake was well off the beaten track and even in the tiny, nearby village, few people knew of its existence.

A few days after my first sight of it, I went back to Rivertree with a rod. I had with me Henry, the club ombudsman. He had been impressed by my florid description of the place yet no doubt he harboured secret doubts. Surely it couldn't have been quite as wonderful as I'd made out? We parked under the trees at the corner of the dam and went and stood on the main landing-stage.

It was one of those hot, drowsy, late-summer afternoons when the air

seems to clot in the stillness and all sounds are reduced to a whisper or a buzz. A bluish haze hung over the bankside trees and the distant hills appeared to be melting in the heat. Nothing moved on the lake except for a sleepy, solitary duck, but we heard a couple of muffled splashes and saw ripples spreading out from beneath an overhanging tree. Before Henry had time to speak, I was hurrying round the bank, rod in hand.

I found the place, a veritable cavern under a great, leaning oak. Shaded from the hot sun were a group of about a dozen carp, just visible in the dappled light. The smallest appeared to be a mere two-pounder and the largest looked as if it might make ten pounds. I tossed in a crust and watched their response. They ignored it. I cast a small piece of bread a few inches in front of the big fish. He nosed forward, sniffed it as delicately as a cat, and backed away as a three-pounder sidled up and took the bait with an ungentlemanly slurp. A short commotion briefly disturbed the peace and then my first Rivertree carp was lying on the bankside grass. A little gem: dark gold flanks, amber belly, midnight-blue back and tail, gill-covers iridescent, like mother of pearl. A few minutes after I'd returned him, Henry grassed another, down by the outfall. It seemed that Rivertree had decided to instantly accept us.

The heat was enough to make a stone sweat. It wasn't just that the temperature was in the mid-eighties, there was that humid, tropical atmosphere. We felt that catching a carp apiece was quite enough exertion for one afternoon, even though the fish had hardly tested our cane. However, after a gentle stroll along the shady banks, making mental notes of the most promising swims, the sun began to lose some of its intensity. We ventured out onto the main landing-stage and fished the open water.

Though the platform jutted only a few yards off the dam wall, sitting on the end of it with a rod was like fishing from the stern of a boat. The lake spread out on three sides and you could drop a bait on a bubbler under your feet or spot a surface-cruising carp hundreds of yards away.

We float fished sweetcorn, after scattering a few handfuls around us, and very pleasant it was to sit and watch a painted quill, hoping for it to become the only animate thing in sight. A few bubbles speckled the surface, then one of the floats slid away sideways and disappeared, and a rod-tip suddenly curved after it. Half a dozen times this happened.

The sun set over the distant hills and a delicious current of cool air began to flow into our faces. As the light faded, the entire lake began to steam and soon the pale mist had thickened and obscured all but the tallest trees. We lost sight of our floats, though it didn't really matter. Henry's rod suddenly clattered across the wooden boards and he grabbed it and found himself playing a very powerful carp. It ran far out into the lake, surfaced with a crash and threw the hook. He didn't even curse. We fished on, holding our rods, and then I too hooked and lost a big fish. But I didn't really mind. We didn't mind about anything. We were supremely content.

Rivertree had proved that we weren't chasing an illusion; it was still possible to find an undisturbed lake that lay, mellow and rich, like old wine, in a changeless landscape.

"You know," said Henry, as I reeled in after my final last cast. "When you were telling me about this place I don't think you did it justice."

22

THE WINCHESTER REQUEST

On 15th December a committee meeting will take place at Isaak Walton's tomb in Winchester Cathedral. The purpose of this meeting is to invite Mr Walton to become a posthumous member. If he agrees we shall automatically elect him to the Pantheon, a shadow committee that we hope will eventually consist of the greatest names in the history of angling.

Supernaturally, there are difficulties. However, we shall suggest to Mr Walton that his reply to us should be in the form of good or bad Omens or Signs. These must be decisive and reasonably spectacular, eg. heavenly voices, a rainbow, a kingfisher or miraculous draught-ale on the one hand; a roll of thunder, a looming cloud, a suspicious policeman or the collapse of the cathedral tower on the other. The committee will wait three hours (after their request) for the manifestation of an Omen, this time to be spent in Winchester or on a nearby river. If, after that time has elapsed, there are no Omens we shall conclude that Mr Walton is considering the matter. We will, in that case, ask for a Sign at a later date.

Trottingshawe has nominated the Long Man of Wilmington for future consideration. Other potential Pantheon members include H. T. Sheringham, A. Ransome, W. Caine, J. Bickerdyke, F. W. K. Wallis, J. Martin, St Peter and Uncle Eddie.

From Flotsam, *the occasional newspaper of the G.S.C.*

THE tower of Winchester Cathedral loomed up into the grey December sky. Apart from the presence of a solitary figure – a man in a pale coat and dark hat – the cathedral grounds were deserted: there were just the bare trees and a few pigeons picking amongst the dead leaves. A clock chimed the hour: twelve noon. The pigeons carried on picking, the solitary figure continued pacing back and forth in front of the tower. At about a quarter past twelve three more figures appeared, coming round from the south side of the building. They approached the other man, who made a gesture of impatience, pointing to his watch. One of the three, quoting a line from a well-known fishing book, said: "Well met, gentlemen: this is lucky that we meet so, just together at this very door." And together the four entered the cathedral.

As unobtrusively as possible, they made their way to Prior Silkstedes Chapel in the South Transept, which contains the tomb of Isaak Walton.

Dandy, Jasper, the author and Parker at Walton's tomb.

Making sure no one had noticed them, they closed the door quietly behind them.

The persons in question were four reasonably compleat anglers from the Golden Scale Club. I should know – I was one of them. The other three were the club chairman, Dandy; the vice-chairman, Jasper; the philologist, Parker. We were visiting the tomb to mark the 299th anniversary of Walton's death.

It was a simple ceremony and, as it began, the cathedral organ struck up a choral, right on cue.

Parker opened a copy of *The Compleat Angler* and received on its pages a token golden hook, but as we took our places, Dandy made a very unfortunate joke. Although neither Jasper nor I were terribly amused by this, Parker went into a fit of hysterical laughter. The Golden Hook was nearly shaken from its page and Dandy showed concern lest the cathedral warden be summoned to 'see what the game was'. Then the laughter subsided, the organist continued playing the choral and the ceremony began properly.

Parker stood at the head of the tomb, Jasper at the foot, Dandy on the left and I on the right. Firstly we paid our respects:

> Gathered at your tomb [I said] are four mortals, fishermen of England and members of the Golden Scale Club. Our second Golden Rule states that we must observe and preserve the traditions of angling as extolled by you and other noble piscators.
>
> Your benevolent presence has often been noted during a day of excellent fishing. It doesn't matter whether this presence springs from memories of your words or from a more celestial source. If a day has been fair we say it has been blessed by the Waltonian Smile and we are thankful. Days that are blank are days of your absence. Ask the chairman, he knows what I mean.
>
> Thus we have come here, on this 299th anniversary, to pay our respects and to present you with this small token as a symbol of that respect.

At this point, Parker offered the hook to Dandy, who passed it to Jasper for inspection. Jasper passed it back to Dandy who then dropped the hook into a small cavity in the tomb, there to lie forever with Isaak's bones.

> We wish to make a humble request [I said]. We would count it a great honour if you would join us not just in spirit but also in name. We ask that you join our club as a member of the Pantheon, a conclave of worthy and honourable anglers who made their mark and then went off to fish more celestial waters. Your name should be at the head of the Pantheon.
>
> Please let us have your reply to our request in the form of an Omen and let that Omen manifest itself either within the next three hours, or when the club next gathers together at some pool or river.
>
> We take our leave of you and will remember your words. We shall be quiet; and go a-angling.

The ceremony concluded, we filed silently out of the glow from the Isaak Walton Window. Eager for an immediate authoritative approval, Dandy and I approached a member of the clergy who happened to be passing by. We told him we'd been paying our respects to Isaak and the clergyman said: "I'm sure that he will be very pleased indeed." I was equally sure that this was a good omen.

We left the cathedral and went for lunch at the Bay Tree Café. No omens. We then visited the Eclipse Inn and ordered four pints of beer. The ale was not memorable, though there had been an eclipse of the sun that morning. But no. This was merely a contrived omen. We left the Eclipse and went into the Vine Inn, which gave a good view of the cathedral. A surly-looking man in a violently green hat came and stood in the gateway to the cathedral grounds.

"What a ghastly hat!" we said, and no sooner were the words uttered than a gust of wind blasted it into the air. The man stood as if spellbound and didn't even turn to see where his hat had landed. It was only when a passer-by came up to him and handed it back that he seemed to come out of his trance. This, surely, was a good omen. However, the ale was again unremarkable. In fact it was almost undrinkable. "It had," said Dandy, "sullied the Sign."

We decided to walk to the River Itchen and see if Isaak would come up with anything in that more appropriate setting. The walk took us round the cathedral and as we passed the Walton Window we heard a choir singing. Then two pigeons flew down and landed on the *centre* of the window-frame. What more could we ask?

The Itchen was running high and, anyway, it was out of season for the trout that Walton fished for; it wasn't surprising that nothing wondrous happened. When the official three hours had elapsed we still couldn't agree that Isaak had accepted our request. I was absolutely convinced, especially after the 'Green Hat Incident' and the 'Window Miracle'. But the others, being naturally sceptical and not a little ungrateful, wanted something more spectacular. Parker insisted that I.W. would answer us properly when we next went fishing.

The twentieth of December was cold, clear, windy and so unsuitable for carp fishing that it seemed ludicrous to even contemplate going. But we did go, for three reasons. Firstly, we had booked a day on Rivertree, and that water had been quite generous with its carp during previous wintry conditions. Secondly, our president – Birtwhistle Ford – had just re-appeared after months chasing silver tourists (salmon) up the Tay: he was eager to cast again into still waters. Thirdly, we were growing impatient over the questions of Isaak's Final Word. We were eager to

go a-fishing and see what, if anything, he had in store for us.

We drove down to Sussex, had a good lunch in the Lickfold Inn and went on to Rivertree. As we approached it, following a long lane that sloped into a wooded valley, the sky clouded over and it began to rain. We caught sight of the water and I said, in a loud voice, "We are here, Isaak, so let us have your sign!" And, as we watched, a rainbow literally grew up out of the field below the dam, arced across the tall oaks and curved directly and vividly into the *centre* of the pool.

23
GOLDEN HOURS

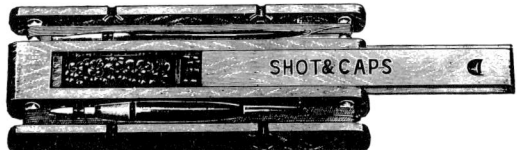

Two days before the new season began Dandy, Parker and I went down to Rivertree. For the first time in the history of the G.S.C. we had planned ahead. We were going to stay at the farmhouse and prepare, at leisure, for the grand opening. The rest of the club would join us on 15th June, by which time we would have baited-up the entire lake and whipped the carp into a frenzy.

Dandy (he was the person you met earlier in the book who used to be called Nick) knocked on the farmhouse door. We received a warm-hearted welcome and were shown to our rooms. After dumping our gear we had a short stroll round the lake and were very pleased to see so many carp bow-waving this way and that across the surface. The sun went down over the hills and we went off for supper and an evening of nostalgic reminiscence. One of the nicest things about times spent fishing in pleasant places with good friends is that when those times have passed you can wax terribly lyrical about them and no one seems to mind. They don't object because they, too, recall those days as if they were savouring vintage port.

The farmhouse was in a deep slumber as we crept away to our respective beds. The atmosphere in any old, quiet house becomes more intense at night, especially so in places with an ancient history. As I sank towards sleep I heard no sound – not even from outside – but I was sure I sensed the presence of someone. Perhaps it was the spirit of an old monk, or maybe it was the spirit of Isaak, come to ensure a prosperous new season.

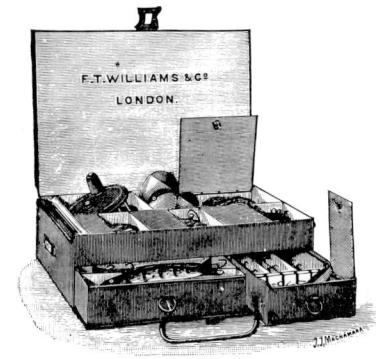

The fifteenth dawned calm and clear and the birds were in raptures about it. We stumbled blearily downstairs at seven-thirty, consumed a magnificent breakfast and then stepped out into the bright morning sunshine.

"How glorious," said Parker, "to be idle all day and not have to bother about chasing carp."

Dandy and I understood his meaning, yet when we strolled across the dam and peered into the water, the sight of a large shadow cruising past made our eyebrows bristle. Immediately we began casting with imaginary rods.

"I think we could at least think about baiting a few swims," I said, and we went off to fetch some bait from the tackle bags. However, when we returned to the dam we had only one can of corn each.

"Is that it?" I asked.

"This is *all* I've got," said Dandy. "For the entire trip."

"It's enough," said Parker, admitting that he too had only brought one can.

"But I thought we were going to come prepared this time," I groaned, "and bait-up the whole lake."

"How many cans have *you* got?" they asked.

We all looked balefully at my tin and I didn't have to say anything. In the end we compromised and baited the lake with half a stale loaf scrounged from the farmhouse.

At noon we drove through five miles of green twisting lanes to a village pub, there to meet Jasper, Henry and Trottingshawe (the treasurer) for lunch. The Black Horse, Byworth, is one of those pubs that used to be common in England; where the landlord never scowls when you stride in with muddy boots, where the beer is real, where the furniture is time-worn and comfortable, where your glass never slides over the polished wooden table because the table has never been polished, where there is no electric 'music' and no slot-machines, where there is a good fire in winter and a bit of garden in summer; in short, a pub that hasn't been polluted by suburban chintz. We tucked into turkey-pie and salad while the landlord, who knew us from previous visits, but who didn't know about close seasons, asked us how the fishing was going. "Ask us again tomorrow!" we said, and raised our glasses to that glorious day.

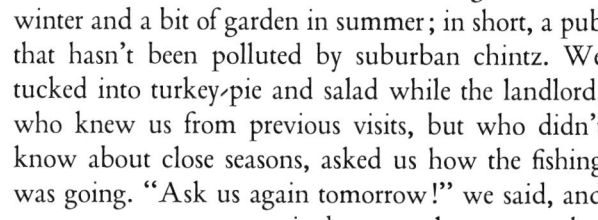

Driving back to Rivertree there were a couple of rod-butts poking out of my van with oddments of wet clothing

GOLDEN HOURS

tied to them. Unfortunately, we'd followed lunch with a stroll along the local river in order to pull faces at the chub, and Dandy had fallen in. (Was it the strength of the ale, or was he pushed?)

We parked at the end of the dam and all but Jasper went to view the lake. He climbed over a gate, inspected a corner of a cornfield where the earth was bare, and then came hurrying back to us.

"Anyone got any rod-rests?" he asked.

We shook out the contents of several canvas holdalls and a revealing collection of bits scattered onto the ground. Apart from the rods, there were several meat-skewers, an arrow, some lengths of copper piping, a gaff, landing-nets, broken pieces of cane, screws, a traditional brass hunting-horn, a golfing brolly, a rolled-up copy of the *Beano*, a festering tweed hat and a can of Newcastle Brown. But no rod-rests.

"Typical!" said Jasper.

I rummaged through the back of my van and, in a tool-chest, found what he wanted. There were two and a half of them.

Jasper grabbed them and marched off. He leaned through the window of his car as he passed it, took out an ancient bat and ball, then went back into the cornfield and, using the rod-rests as stumps, paced out a cricket pitch. There was an acre of unsown ground, where the farmer had, in fact, suggested we park our cars, and here we spent the afternoon, bowling each other out. Parker and Trottingshawe proved to be the handiest with the bat, scoring innumerable sixes, putting at least one dent in a car roof and nearly braining a cow. Birtwhistle arrived in the middle of the match and it was his deadly spin that destroyed both champions and the rod-rests.

With the match over, we congratulated Jasper on his interesting choice of pitch. What had made it so tricky to play on was the fact that it was ploughed.

Skeffingdon Dolrimple (vintner), our youngest member, had been unlucky enough to be sitting his A-level Science exam that morning. When he'd as good as finished, he just grabbed his rods and tackle, jumped on a train and got from Yeovil to Haslemere by tea time. The message reached me that he was waiting for collection. I drove off to fetch him and while I was away four more members turned up. Algy Selwood (aviator), Derbyshire Ball (sub-archivist), Jardine Hassan (overseas correspondent) and Cousin Jeremy (associate member). It was just as well we had five acres of lake to ourselves. Had there been the same turn-out at a populous day-ticket water, opening night might have degenerated into civil war.

Before the sun had set everyone had decided on their pitch for the night. No one had brought any great quantities of corn but there was enough to sprinkle a good helping into every swim. Almost immediately there were bubbly signs that the carp were feeding. In one shallow area it was possible to see the bow-waves homing in on the free offerings. We set up rods and nets, ready for midnight, then departed to the inn at the nearby village of Lickfold.

Somehow we all managed to cram round a single table in a large inglenook fireplace. We ordered food and a gallon and a half of ale and for half an hour or so there was reasonable quiet, apart from the clattering of knives and forks and the clinking of glasses. But then someone remembered that we had yet to hold an Annual General Meeting and as most members present were those with a terrible aversion for official functions...

By the time the chairman had been dishonourably expelled three times and then elected to the chair 'beyond life, beyond death', the other customers were looking uneasy. By the time the vice-chairman had gaffed the treasurer 'for not wearing a tie on the opening night', the landlord was looking longingly at the clock. But then the president, in reply to a question about the Pantheon, confirmed that he *had* witnessed Isaak's rainbow. Thus we were reminded of Isaak's motto, Study to be Quiet. The atmosphere calmed, the landlord returned to his pumps, the other customers returned to their conversations and Algy said he'd save his maiden speech till next time.

At 11.30 a crescent moon was hanging like a gold sabre over the western end of the lake. The moon and stars were perfectly reflected in the still surface and apart from the occasional splash of a leaping carp the night was silent.

We boiled some kettles for tea. The air was chilly and we felt the need of a hot drink before the first cast. A few minutes before midnight, twelve anglers crept quietly away under the dark of the bankside trees and settled down in their pitches. I imagined the diabolic atmosphere at all the other carp lakes we used to know: the flashing of torches, the blinking of little red lights and, above all, the persistent bleeping of the electronic bite-indicators. At Rivertree there were no torches, no lights and no bleeps. However, there was a single blast on a traditional brass hunting-horn, signalling midnight and the opening of the new season.

One for each chime of a distant church clock, twelve lots of tackle plopped into the lake. Then an expectant hush, followed after a quarter of an hour by a sharp splash and the rasp of a reel. Who was it? I wondered. Who had been chosen by Isaak to be First Man? It was Skeffingdon Dolrimple, justly rewarded for skimping an A-level in pursuit of a nobler cause. A few minutes later, in a gap in the trees along the north bank, my own line began to run out and I hooked the second of the season, though Trottingshawe insists it was the third.

By one o'clock it appeared that a miracle was happening and that,

for the first time in history, we would all catch an opening-day carp. Ten fish had been landed by then and although they weren't evenly distributed, it surely wouldn't be long before everyone had enjoyed some sport. But then a cold mist began to blot out the reflected stars and the temperature plunged. Those of us under the sheltering trees didn't suffer as much as the four anglers fishing on the exposed landing-stages, off the dam. In the silence I was sure I could hear the merry chattering of teeth. The lake went dead and it was a good excuse to get the kettle on the boil again.

At about 4 a.m. the light began to grow in the north-east. The first bird to greet the new day was a cuckoo. A swallow was next, twittering from somewhere high above the lake, then a skylark began to warble and a pigeon cooed. Colour began to seep into the landscape, though it would be a long time before we saw the sun. And as the light increased so the fish began to feed again.

A carp showed contempt for my carefully judged sidestrain. After turning his flank towards me, he did a quick half-circle and almost flew out into the lake. I was using a sweetly geared pre-war Altex and its clutch whined beautifully.

After five minutes, though, I realised I would never get that fish in quietly – or rather, I would never get *those* fish in quietly. My carp had crossed the president's line and he was also attached to something lively. He was twenty yards along the bank and must have been using stouter tackle than me. After a while, however hard I pulled, it seemed the carp's cradle was going his way. I listened to the familiar grating of his reel, then heard his distinctive chuckle. He informed me that he'd only managed to get one carp into his net. It wasn't mine. My fish had somehow managed to throw the hook.

Algy, Jeremy, Parker and Derbyshire were the shivering anglers fishing off the dam. They were hidden by a layer of mist but, as I watched, the mist thinned and they gradually emerged through it. I saw Parker, on the centre staging, strike and hook a fish. It was all very distant, but the carp seemed to make quite a fuss and it was a long time before I saw the net going in. Then, on either side of him, the others politely applauded. From what I could gather, it was a good fish, but this didn't matter; it was more significant that Parker was using a very famous old carp rod that the club had recently acquired. Now he'd christened it in his own name. A few minutes after this incident Derby landed two fish in quick succession. Algy was sitting on the end of a platform we called

Parker caning them at Rivertree.

Berol's Boards, with his feet dangling in the water and a rather despondent droop about his shoulders. Jeremy was fishing next to him, looking more perky, and so it wasn't difficult to deduce their catch. Jeremy: some; Algy: none. Just as I was thinking about taking a stroll to see what else was happening my silver foil hissed sharply at me and I hooked another carp. Instead of driving away in the usual wildie manner this fish held its ground and merely swayed heavily first one way, then the other. I was using a Mk IV Avon, with six-pound line, and for some time it just quivered in a critical bend. I thought I'd hooked a monster. Slowly it came in, making furls and vortices on the surface, but when I netted it and heaved it up it didn't look much bigger than five pounds. I've had twenty-pounders that were smaller in spirit.

At eight-thirty the hunting horn again echoed across the lake and

minutes later we were all trudging like a victorious army across the dam. The farmer's wife, bless her heart, had agreed to provide everyone with breakfast yet the sight of us approaching the farmhouse door, pale, weary and very hungry, must have tempted her to change her mind. However, the door opened straight away and we were greeted with a welcoming smile. We sat down at two large tables, and never has a breakfast been more earnestly consumed.

Only as we began to relax after the meal could we begin to properly digest what had happened beforehand. It was clear that things had gone rather against the grain. Thinking back, we couldn't remember an opening night that had seen more than two brace of carp, and never, as I have said, had we managed a fish apiece. Indeed, the chairman is famous for having once fished through an entire season without catching anything.

It's true, we are always pleased to catch *something* – but *sixty-three* carp, *before* breakfast! Since midnight, Dandy had caught more carp than he'd landed during the previous ten years. Trottingshawe, who had grassed the most, complained of aching wrists.

The only members to conform to tradition were Jardine, Henry, Algy and Jasper. Jardine had chosen the one dud pitch on the whole lake and Henry had been asleep all night. Poor Algy had to leave before breakfast to fly a jumbo to Geneva. He had landed a fish in the end, but unfortunately it was rather small and so although he said how much he'd enjoyed himself, we still felt sorry for his passengers. Jasper had caught one carp during the first hour, then he unrolled his sleeping-bag and wasn't heard of again until lunch-time.

Things were less hectic during the day and most of us were able to put up a second rod and enjoy a spot of float fishing. By tea-time the carp total had risen to an embarrassing seventy-five.

"What's happened?" asked an astonished Parker. "I thought this was meant to be a club of reasonably straight rods."

"That was before Isaak joined us," I said.

24
PARKER'S BAG

I cut out a cardboard carp, tied it to the line from a centre-pin reel and lowered it out of my bedroom window so that it hung about six feet from the ground. Then I went to sleep. At first light, the reel screamed and I leapt out of bed. Jasper, calling to collect me, had seen the carp and given it a tug.

"It's more original than an alarm clock," I croaked, as I looked blearily out of the window.

There was no time for breakfast, though I snatched a cup of tea. I grabbed my bundle of rods, threw a few bits of tackle into a big bag, stole a loaf from the kitchen and away we went, driving through deserted lanes to one of our favourite waters.

The surface of the lake was almost invisible beneath its veil of mist; in the east the trees appeared hard and black against the increasing glow; all other details in the landscape were half-obscured by the combination of mist, dew and shadow. A fish leapt, making a big splash that we didn't see, but which sounded, in the midst of the dawn chorus, like a cymbal crash. The ripples spread, unseen under the mist, till they shuffled the reeds at our feet.

It was the perfect carp-fisher's dawn.

Jasper crept off one way, I crept the other. We had the lake to ourselves,

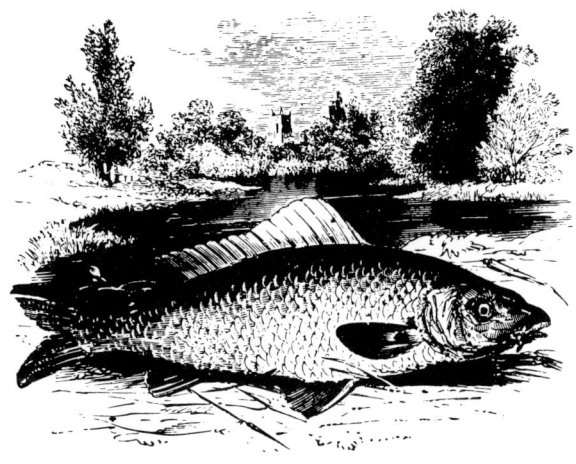

though it was a club water. And we had the world to ourselves, though it was a Monday and we should have been working. "What do we need to make money for?" we said. "This midsummer morning is free, all we need is the time to be in it." Out went the offerings of loose crust and, within minutes, there was some enthusiastic clooping. Over in the weed bed, a bit of bread disappeared into a funnel-shaped mouth. I baited a size 6 hook with a crust the size of a matchbox and flicked it out. Two other free offerings went down before the carp approached the bait. He bumped it with his nose, turned, circled, sniffed again then just hung there, looking. His confidence and his appetite grew. He pushed the bread once, then took it in a single gulp. I waited until the line was slithering across the surface and then gave the rod a bang.

Whee! Scraps of weed and a gallon of water went skyward as the fish slashed the surface with his tail and plunged straight down. He stuck for a few seconds, in among the tangled stems, then bolted clear and, luckily for me, launched himself into the open water.

When I saw him roll, just off the net, I thought I'd got a ten-pound wildie, but it didn't make any difference to my enjoyment when the scales read two pounds less.

So dawn became morning. A breeze drove the mist away, the first ripples appeared on the surface and the first drone of 'civilisation' sounded from a mile-distant road. The sun grew warmer, but the carp continued to feed. Jasper got two nice specimens on flake and I had another on crust – a four-pounder. Still we had the lake to ourselves, so we decided to fish on until our solitude was disturbed. As the day progressed, I began to wish I'd brought something to eat. It's always the same whenever I go fishing. I'm so keen to get to the waterside that I've only ever got time to grab the essentials of tackle. I would explode with frustration if I had to spend even five minutes making a sandwich or a flask of tea. After four hours' fishing I normally start complaining to myself for being so disorganised and impatient. I tell myself that it *is* humanly possible to prepare a packed lunch before setting out – have I not seen, with my own eyes, anglers arriving at the bankside laden not only with enough hardware to start a tackle shop but with enough food to open a restaurant?

It wouldn't be so bad if I could count on my friends, but while they're often good for a spare hook or float, or some bait, it's rare for any of them to have even so much as a packet of crisps.

I tried to overcome my hunger by concentrating on a difficult cast. There was a carp in a small lily bed not far from the inlet stream. To reach it, I had to drop a crust over a tall bed of reeds, being careful not to overcast into another reed bed just beyond the lilies. After three attempts, the bait landed in the right place and, within seconds, the carp took it down with a casual gulp. As I hauled, he dived towards me and locked himself snugly in the nearest reed clump. I had to call Jasper to help; he waded out and, somehow, got the bounder in the net.

"Hardly worth it," he said, looking down at a three-pounder.

"Never mind that," I replied, "have you got anything to eat?"

"Afraid not."

"What! Nothing?"

"I suppose we could bake the carp," he said.

"That's almost cannibalism," I said, "and anyway, we've got no chips."

We knew we'd quietly starve to death if we fished on, but fish on we did, for the carp were still frisky and we hoped we might contact one of the elusive monsters. An hour later I saw an apple pie surfacing in a weed bed. Jasper said his casting had improved enormously since he discovered that the pond was stocked with chocolate Swiss rolls. But he couldn't hook them. I said we'd better go home.

A few weeks later, four of us set out on an epic trip to a South Wales carp lake. Naturally, we were well supplied with tackle and, of course, we took provisions – but not enough to last. We'd planned to fish for

Carps and Beer

Parker's Bag

Barbel fishing on the Hampshire Avon.

nine days, yet after three we'd eaten everything, and after five we'd spent all our money. On the sixth day the carp's hunger was so great we forgot about our own, but on the seventh we knew we'd have to resort to drastic measures. So, in the morning, after a cup of black tea, we had to forgo the carp and set off to the local river for some trout.

Trout fishing on the Ithon was not very remarkable that season. In fact we felt sorry for any regular bona-fide trout fisher. After all, if four hardened (starving) carp-fishers could manage only one trout between them, and that on a worm, what hope was there for the dry-fly purist?

It was my brother, Nick, who got the fish and it wasn't nearly big enough to share. We watched him as he gutted, cleaned and cooked it over a small fire. But we couldn't watch him eat it.

The next day, I remembered Captain Oates. He was the valiant member of Scott's Antarctic expedition who went out alone into the blizzards so that the rest of the team might survive on the dwindling supplies. I followed Oates' gallant example, setting out from the lakeside tent in the early morning so that the others might better sustain themselves on the few remaining tea-bags and one stale loaf. I hitch-hiked home and spent the next night in the larder.

On the last day in September, a few seasons later, Jasper again called for me at dawn. Barbel were our quarry and we got down to the Avon near Ringwood just as the sun was rising. A lovely morning, the meadows sparkling with dew, the air warm and moist and the river reflecting the first tints of autumn.

At about nine o'clock, we noticed a familiar figure approaching across the fields. As he drew nearer we could see he was traditionally attired, looking in fact like a typical Golden Scale Club member, in his Norfolk jacket, Irish-tweed hat and heavy brogues. He had a cane rod in one hand, a capacious landing-net in the other and a game-bag slung over his shoulder. There was, however, one jarring feature in his appearance. In his left hand, together with the net, he was clutching a large, white polythene bag.

"Salutations, noble Parker!" we said.

"Greetings, fellow barbel-baiters!" he replied.

"What's in the bag?" I asked.

"Not telling," came the reply.

We fished quite hard throughout that day. I explored a jungle of overgrown bank, fishing places you had to crawl to or climb into before you could cast. I found a formidable-looking swim where the current took

Parker's Bag

The contemplative moment and tea by the river.

the bait round and beneath a massive half-submerged willow. First cast I got a tremendous whiplash of a bite and just clamped down on it and tried to hold it. For a few seconds it seemed I was winning, then the fish just rose into the trailing branches and snagged me solid. Jasper, fishing small baits, had a few chub and a beautiful two-pound grayling. Parker failed to land a fish though, like me, he had his chances.

As I said, we had worked hard at the river, and around tea-time, I began to feel that familiar, gnawing hunger; once more I began to crave for things other than fish. I struggled back through the jungle and trudged upstream to where Jasper was fishing. Imagine my delight when I saw a kettle boiling merrily on the bank.

"I suppose you haven't got anything to go with this?" queried Jasper, as he prepared three mugs of tea.

"Don't even mention food," I said, "we might start hallucinating again."

Parker, hearing the clink of tea-things, came down the bank carrying his plastic bag. "It's a present from the Captain," he said (the Captain is his remarkable wife). As he unwrapped it, the sun broke from behind a haloed cloud, barbel began leaping in the river, voles skipped arm in arm along the bank, a swan sang an operatic aria, bells began to chime and all the grasshoppers in the field burst into spontaneous applause.

It was a plum-cake.

PART V

Redmire Revisited

In the heat of noonday I have cruised in a punt upon the surface of that small fathomless pool and looked far down among waving weed cables at broad netted backs stirring there in those mysterious depths . . .

Bigger carp than Walker's will be caught: indeed any day we may hear of a fifty-pounder . . .

'B.B.' Confessions of a Carp Fisher (1970) (2nd edn)

I LEFT Redmire at the end of 1973. I was loath to do it, not only because I'd be giving up what was then the best carp fishing in the country, but also because I'd be saying farewell to Rod Hutchinson and Bob Jones. Rod was the greatest and most original carp-angler I have ever met; he was also daft, which is why we fished so well together. Bob was a more orthodox angler, but he was only slightly less eccentric a person than Rod, and what is more, he could make a better cup of tea.

There were various reasons for giving up the 'mire' but the most important was that simple fact, mentioned before – I was obsessed by it. Everything else had become subordinate to it. Fishing one week in three, the fortnight between visits was a kind of limbo in which I did virtually nothing. I lost interest in most of my old carp ponds, I lost touch with most of my old carp-angling pals. Naturally, I hardly considered work and was therefore penniless. Redmire was replacing reality, so I had to banish myself from it. It wasn't so much the sensible thing to do, more a question of survival.

It was a relief in the end. Obsession is bad for the soul. Also, I left at a good time, having got the measure of the place and being fairly sure I could always catch carp there. There was one other thing, though it might sound like a contradiction. I may have lost my heart to it, but after two years Redmire's magic had definitely faded, as magic does when it becomes familiar.

By 1977 I cannot say that I had become more sensible or had 'grown up', but I was steadier on my feet, having established that I could make enough money to live, simply by taking a camera with me on my wanderings. It seemed, also, that I was still in love with Redmire, for when I was suddenly offered a return ticket I gladly accepted. I knew I'd cured my obsession so it would be safe to go back. The offer arose as a result of a rather unfortunate argument between Tom Mintram, who then ran

Redmire, and a bunch of mutineers. Luckily, Tom won the battle of words hands down, but subsequently found himself with a few holes in his syndicate. It was one of these holes that I now happily filled.

Long before the mutiny, and much to my disappointment, Rod and Bob had left Redmire. But Henry* joined the group with me and for the first season I'd be fishing with him and Ron Lally, both of them great characters and good company. (As they had less free time than me, half my Redmire days would be solitary ones – not that I minded.)

The only regret I had when I stood once more on the dam was that I'd seen Redmire in its glory and now, after the terrible elm-plague and the death of the great willow, it would never look quite as lovely again.

But even with half the tree cover gone the atmosphere had not changed. Redmire has an atmosphere, a 'mood', that is unique and quite powerful. It is not sinister, like some old deep lakes but, especially in the late evenings or before sunrise, it is brooding and mysterious. Anyone who knows its name is obviously aware of its history and this lends a great deal to the mood of the place, as if you could sense all the dreams of the generations of Redmire fishermen. It always surprises me to hear of some anglers who say they can't appreciate this atmosphere.

Also the smell of the place had not changed. Like every carp water I know, Redmire has its own individual scent, a scent that, in summer, is made up almost entirely of the perfume that wafts from the twin balsam poplars on the east bank.

Returning to Redmire I was like a pilgrim visiting Mecca for the second time. As I said, I felt that I'd got the measure of the place. Also I was less concerned than before about actually catching fish, content for most of the time in just letting the surroundings grow up around me. Living quietly, a week at a time, on the bank I felt that time was not actually passing, but collecting, like snow. It's hard to describe how perfect it seemed to live utterly simply beside that quiet pool. If the weather was fine I slept under the stars and never bothered with setting up canvas. I washed in the outfall stream, made tea with the Redmire water, read books in the shade of the oaks, spent hours up treetops watching the carp through binoculars and went for long walks over the surrounding fields. I even conversed at length with the Redmire owls. Sometimes I enjoyed myself so much *not* fishing that I wondered why I need trouble myself

---

*Henry had one ambition: to catch a Redmire carp. He caught four, all over twenty pounds, and then, satisfied, left the syndicate.

with rods and reels. It was always a wrench to stow my gear and leave for home. At that time the life of a country tramp seemed the life of Riley.

But every so often the tranquil mood would change and I'd feel the pool making a kind of challenge. It was challenging me to break its hold over the monsters. I'd see them then, basking near the surface or pushing through deep weed beds, and whenever they appeared I stopped flitting about and became, for a while, a serious angler.

25

THE MONSTERS OF THE MYTH

By the end of the drought summer of 1976, Redmire had shrunk to just a small, deep pool, with most of the carp milling around near the surface. Everyone became extremely concerned but the fish survived until September, when the rains came at last and the pool re-filled. That fallowing of a large expanse of lake bed had a remarkable effect on Redmire. By June 1977 the water was clearer and purer than I'd ever seen it. The weed was bright green and lush and even the oldest and weariest of the carp discovered a new lease of life. Creeping round the shallows when the fish were feeding, I saw several of my old friends, recognisable by scale patterns or coloration or a distinctive body-shape. They were all blooming. There was one mirror in particular, a large sandy-coloured fish, which really staggered me. I'd seen it three years before, in my own landing-net, when it weighed thirty-eight pounds. At that time it looked pale and jaded, like an ancient man who'd lived all his life in a cave. I thought it was on its last fins and put it straight back without photographing it. Now here it was again, right in front of me as I watched from an island. Its pale flanks had become a deep, rich ochre, the mottled grey back now looked plum-coloured and I guessed it would probably weigh about forty-five pounds. The pectorals quivered and it balanced itself with surprising delicacy as it turned to face me. Even the head was different; rounder, less prehistoric-looking. I flicked a bean in front of it and it took it on the drop.

Quickly, I went to fetch my rod and when I got back the fish was still there. I tossed in a few more beans, then swung out a bait to land just in front of it. It picked up some of the free offerings, but then turned and swam ten yards further out. Down went its nose again and, moments later, a pale cloud of disturbed mud began to billow around it. It was obviously hungry, visibly feeding, so I reeled in, re-baited, and, after taking very careful aim, re-cast. I was using a quarter-ounce Arlesey Bomb and it landed directly on the fish's head! Exit, rapidly, one monster carp and it was two years before I saw it again.

That was the first time I'd seen a Redmire carp that looked clearly over the record. During his years at the pool, Rod had spotted *five* such

fish and seen one so big that it boggled his mind. I'd spent just as much time as he had up trees, watching through binoculars and polarising glasses, but the times when the monsters appeared were few and I always missed them. I certainly did not disbelieve Rod's stories; there was too much about them to be fantasies. Also there were other anglers who had been looking in the right direction at the right time and had seen something to almost stop their hearts.

Eventually, one warm August day, a monster finally appeared in front of my eyes. On the morning of that day the wind had been blowing crazily from all points of the compass. The fish were chivvied about by the gusts like worried sheep. Gradually, the wind lessened and steadied and became a gentle easterly breeze. The carp moved down to the dam end of the pool and took up exactly the same individual positions in the weed beds as they had earlier in the week. I'd never seen, or rather, never before noticed a group of carp returning to a recognisable formation. All these fish were twenty-pounders and they lay basking just below the surface in a big weed bed under the dam wall. As I looked at them I saw that the overall design they made was not, after all, quite the same as before. There was an addition. On the far side of the weeds, lying broadside to me, was an enormous common carp. It was the biggest freshwater fish I had ever seen, yet even though it shook me, I was absolutely convinced that it was *not* the king. The few anglers who had seen the king all stressed that its size was beyond belief. This other fish was certainly big, but it was credible.

It was about twenty yards out and it dwarfed all the other carp, even though they were much nearer to me. Like a battleship swinging at anchor, it turned slowly until it was lying head-on. Then it appeared even more huge, for I could see the tremendous girth.

How big? It looked as large as a bull amongst a herd of calves. How heavy? Even using the other fish as yardsticks I could only make a rough guess, but it couldn't have weighed much less than fifty-five pounds and may have been ten pounds more.

In the autumn of that same year, I saw another monster. It was during the last week of October and I'd been fishing alone, through days of cold weather without seeing so much as a bubble of interest from the fish. On the Saturday afternoon the temperature rose and the sun shone through the hazy cloud. Once again I climbed my look-out tree – an alder on one of the islands – and scanned the pool for signs of life. A common carp of about eighteen pounds appeared, then two more, a little larger. Together, they began to go up towards the shallows but, as they passed my tree, there was a strengthening of the breeze. It was blowing down towards the dam and they turned with it and went back into the deeps.

About thirty yards out, in four or five feet of water, there was a pale cloud of mud with a vague dark shape in the middle of it. At first I thought this shape was a fish, but then decided it couldn't possibly be. It was too big. It was probably a decaying weed bed. I looked away to see if there were any carp elsewhere and when I glanced back the dark mass was slowly moving forward, rising up out of the pale cloud and coming nearer. It *was* a carp. Once it was clear of the mud cloud its outline became more sharply defined and it didn't then appear quite so colossal. But it was still huge, quite as big as that monster by the dam and yet obviously a different fish. It was a strangely dark – almost jet black – leather carp.

A 1934 Hardy Victor bends into a big Redmire carp.

It sank slowly back to the bottom and as it lay there it fanned quite violently with its pectorals and soon a pale cloud of mud had billowed up around it, almost engulfing it. It was as if a black air-ship was hiding in the middle of a small puffy cloud. After five minutes, it rose up again, turned round and drifted fifteen yards down the pool. Then it sank to the bottom again and swept up another mud cloud. I've seen carp perform all kinds of strange tricks, but never anything like that. It wasn't grubbing about with its nose, merely fanning the silt and sucking in the shrimps and worms that it disturbed, like a whale filtering plankton.

I must have watched that giant for nearly half an hour before I realised that it was gradually leap-frogging its way towards my baited swim. It was about to find itself drifting over a mouth-watering bed of fresh cockles. I monkeyed down the tree and hurried back to my rods which were at Inghams, half way between the island and the dam. Quickly I baited a hook and cast well out, over to my left. After scattering a few more cockles over the bait, I cast a second straight out. Within minutes the line on the right-hand rod began to trickle through the rings. I struck and reeled in an extremely tactless eel. Then the other line began to run out and I locked the rod into an amazing bend. It was a 1934 Hardy

Victor — a sea-trout rod — and its tip almost blurred into invisibility as it quivered above the water. The clutch began to click off the yards, and, as the fish trundled towards the far bank, I knew it had to be the giant.

Years before, at Llandrindod Wells, I accidentally hooked a motorboat which steadily unwound two hundred yards of line from my reel. The gradual, unhurried pull, sustained to the line's last inch, was not, I thought, something you would normally experience in fishing, unless a whale picked up your bait. But the slow ponderous hauling of that Redmire carp was exactly the same as the drag of the chugging motorboat, and not dissimilar, I bet, to the pull of a whale. I'd experienced a few tremendous battles at Redmire with some magnificent fish, but the initial runs were always either fast and furious or faltering and erratic, nothing as deliberate and sullen as this.

It was as if the fish had merely decided to go for a long leisurely stroll. It was swimming in a dead straight line, yet after three or four minutes it seemed it must surely have reached the far bank and was now bulldozing its way across the fields. The reel kept ticking and I kept glancing anxiously at the spool, wondering how many yards I'd got left (the line was eight pounds breaking-strain). Finally the fish came to a kind of juddering halt and the rod thumped a couple of times. Right under the opposite bank I saw, to my amazement, a sudden huge expanse of bubbles. The carp must have been ploughing through the marginal silt. Then, even at such a distance, I clearly saw an enormous dorsal rise slowly up and sink down again.

With the fish on one side of the pool and me on the other we seemed to have reached an impasse, though I could tell the carp hadn't anchored itself immovable. I noticed the way of the line was stretched parallel across the surface. A moorhen could have tight-roped along it from bank to bank. The bend decreased slightly in the rod and I wound in a few yards, then a few more. Then everything was gliding and effortless as the fish planed across the deep channel. The place opposite me was known as Pitchfords Pit, the deepest hole in Redmire. The carp floated over this hole and then seemed to propel itself into it. The angle of the line steepened, the rod curved after it, the reel began to sing; then the whole landscape jerked back from me and though I wound frantically it kept falling further and further away. . .

The loss of any big fish always leaves a slightly bitter taste in the mouth, but the taste soon fades, especially if you can be philosophical. It's hard, though, to be philosophical when you have just lost one of the biggest

The consolation common – a splendid-looking sixteen-and-a-half-pounder.

carp in England. (It was a certain, over-springy make of French hook that had failed me. I never used them again.)

As a small consolation, I soon hooked another fish – on the same vintage rod – and, after a few minutes, netted a sixteen-and-a-half-pounder that was the brightest and most classically proportioned common carp I've ever seen.

After the incident with that dark-coloured monster I began to use the names of chess pieces to describe the Redmire aristocracy. The big leather I called the Black Queen, the monster by the dam was the Knight. The forty-five-pound mirror was the Bishop and of course there was the King. The pawns were the ordinary twenty- and thirty-pounders. To complete the set I needed a Castle and in 1979, I eventually discovered a fish fit for the title.

The Monsters of the Myth

I was fishing then with Barry Mills* and it was he who first spotted the 'new' monster. He was watching carp from the branches of the big oak, in the Evening Pitch, and he suddenly called for me to join him. As we perched, twenty feet above deep, clear water, there were three fish basking below us. The smallest was a leather that we knew weighed thirty pounds (Barry had caught it the previous season), the middle-sized one was the Bishop and the largest was a massive, slate-grey mirror carp, at least six inches longer than the Bishop and much broader and deeper. It was very, very ancient looking and so 'The Castle' seemed an appropriate name. I should think it weighed not less than sixty pounds.

Barry had spent two seasons keeping hawk-like watch for one of the giants and, in his quiet way, he was obviously awestruck. At the time, it was fashionable to pooh-pooh the old Redmire legends and one or two articles had appeared in the angling press stating that Redmire was finished as a big fish water.

"It's a shame," said Barry, as the Castle drifted under our noses, "that the sceptics can't see this."

We watched it for half an hour, then it sank into invisibility and we never saw it again.

The monsters' extreme elusiveness is perhaps Redmire's strangest mystery and, apart from sudden changes in weather conditions, there seems to be no rhyme or reason to their brief, sudden appearance after months, or even years, of concealment. Richard Walker told me that he used to see the monsters quite regularly until the big freeze-up of 1963 when they seemed to go into retirement. In fact Walker and his friends thought for a while that the giants had all died. After 1963 they were seen only very rarely. Then came the drought of 1976. No one actually saw anything very large during that period – which seems odd – but afterwards the giants began to rise again from their deep hiding places, tempted into the shallows, no doubt, by the new sweetness of the water.

The accumulated silt of several centuries had, in a single summer, been dried out by the sun and wind. When the rains came Redmire was rejuvenated.

By the end of 1979 I was convinced that I'd seen all the monsters that

---

*Barry was the epitome of Walton's contemplative angler. A good naturalist, too, with a deep respect for the wild inhabitants of the waterside. I once saw him give up a chance for a thirty-pound carp when he discovered a fly-catcher's nest in the tree he was about to cast from.

remained in Redmire. I had seen the Bishop, the Castle, the Black Queen, *two* Knights and finally the King himself. The King was not dead and I could now count myself among the lucky few who'd been honoured by his presence.

It was in July of 1979 and the weather had been hot and sultry for days. Only during the last hours of evening would the carp appear, swimming leisurely up from the deep weed beds and drifting out onto the shallows. Not long before sunset, on the third of the month, I again began to fish, casting into a cave of overhanging branches near the top of the pool, on the east bank. Before my float had even had time to settle it vanished and I quickly bundled an eight-pounder into the net. Fish four times his size were moving past me and I soon dropped another bait back into the pool, casting now from a gap between two willows. A good fish, over twenty pounds, went down under the float and in a moment the quill was almost engulfed by a froth of bubbles. I sat ready to strike, but the fish was obviously avoiding the bait.

Three more big carp appeared, coming round the willow branches and under two small patches of weed. As they swam into open water they coalesced into one stupendous fish. I had to shake my head. It was impossible. Had someone dropped a dolphin into Redmire? It shadowed past me, about twenty feet away, and I plainly saw the immense size of the fins and tail and the great scales across the shoulders, each one as large as the palm of my hand. This was the indisputable King, floating through the crystal-clear water, like a planet drifting through its galaxy.

I can't say how heavy I thought it was, but Rod's description of it fits perfectly. It *did* look as big as a man.

To add to the magnificence – and strangeness – of the spectacle, two other huge fish followed in his majesty's train. Like the King, they were fully scaled and I'm convinced that one of them was the monster I'd seen from the dam in 1977. They were identical to each other in size, shape and colour, being roughly forty inches long, gracefully proportioned and very dark along the back. They were giants yet, incredibly, as they dwarfed the twenty-pounder under my float, so they were dwarfed in turn by the Leviathan.

Had all my wildest fishing dreams been rolled into one splendid extravaganza it would never have matched the sight that was passing in front of my eyes. The King and his two Knights slowly disappeared into the reflected sunset, going on to the feeding grounds at the very top of the pool. As the water became thick with dense clouds of red mud, I crept round onto Wasp Island, near the feeder stream. The water rocked and heaved, gently washing at the roots under my feet. Now and then a great fin or an enormous shiny back would rise above the surface. With trembling hand (and using my strongest tackle), I cast and then sat feverish, from sunset to midnight, without so much as a shiver on the line. It was a relief when I finally decided to reel in. Not only was it terrifying to fish for such creatures, it also seemed irreverent.

Lying in my sleeping-bag later that night, I looked towards the moon as it went down across the pool, but saw only the King, passing again and again in front of the willows.

26

THE MYSTERY OF THE REDMIRE TEAPOT

ON the last day of the 1979–80 season I was fishing alone at Redmire. The weather was cold and windy and the sky clear and bright. I was pitched under the oaks, but for twenty-four hours the lines had not tightened once. The water temperature was too low for the carp's comfort and they had, seemingly, gone back into their winter dreams.

About four o'clock in the afternoon, as I looked across the water, a dark, rounded shape suddenly appeared, rising up almost in the pool's centre. It remained floating on the surface, drifting with the wind towards the dam. I thought a small carp must have died (of cold) and had rolled belly-up to the top. I went onto the dam to have a closer look and as it approached I could see that it wasn't a carp. It looked like an old tin can. Then it washed ashore and I picked it up. It wasn't a carp or a tin can. It was a very ancient, brown china teapot.

This teapot had, I guessed, belonged to one of the first carp-fishers to throw a line at Redmire. I could imagine what had happened. Dick Walker had just landed his forty-four-pound carp. Such was his jubilation that he grabbed the first thing that came to hand – a brown china teapot – and, whooping with joy, hurled it far out into the pool. For twenty-eight years it had lain on the bottom, with great carp cruising over it and leeches making a home inside it. And then, on the last day of the 1979–80 season, something happened (gas bubbles?) to make it rise to the surface and drift, upside down, to the bank.

I took the pot and jammed it into the branches of a willow, right up at the head of the pool. It seemed the proper thing to do.

Of course, whether this was Walker's teapot or not, it was absurd to think there was something significant in the way it rose, like Excalibur, to the surface. But one or two other odd things had been happening. For instance: dreams of splendid portent; a rod coming into my hands that had been made twenty-five years before, by Walker himself; the last words of Jack the Roadman before we said goodbye for that season: "When you come back, you get that big one. *You get 'im!*" He'd never said anything like that before. Then Jardine telephoned me, after months of silence, and said I would catch a monster when the new season began.

It was enough to make you look out for black cats, or magpies, or horse-shoes, or even brown china teapots.

My next fishing day at Redmire would be the first day of the new season. By the time I set off, on 15th June, I was convinced, stupidly convinced, that I was about to break the old carp record. I had never had this feeling before and I had certainly never said anything of the sort before. But a vague premonition had grown stronger – so strong, in fact, that before I left for Redmire I posted two cards, one to my brother, the other to one of my best friends. I'd written that I was about to catch a fish over forty-four pounds.

On the first day of the season, as I drew my Walker-built rod from its holdall, Jack the Roadman was waiting to hear my news, two other people had already received it, and a teapot was jammed in a willow tree by the feeder stream.

27

A RECORD CARP STORY

TWO versions of this story have been published before. One I wrote for *Angling* (September 1980) and the other was part of a letter I wrote to 'B.B.' and which he included in his new edition of *Confessions* and in his book *The Quiet Fields*. The version I include here is the original, straight from the weather-beaten pages of my fishing diary.

Packed the van after breakfast (on the 15th) with the Gaffer ensuring I had all the small things I usually forget. Eventually left home at 2.30. The newly acquired van (another battered old Renault) purred along, uncomplaining, down the twisting green roads for the 120 miles to Bernithan Court. I parked in the old enclosure, well out of sight from the pool, and then went and had tea with Barry and John (John Carver). We discussed prospects and generally agreed that they were promising. The pool was quite free of weed, the fish were moving and conditions, weatherwise, were ideal. I went up to the shallows with Barry and, as we perched in a willow, Barry pointed to a big fish. But the angle of light was straight between my eyes and I didn't see it.

Later on, as we sat talking in the old pump-house, a tumultuous downpour broke over the pool and hammered deafeningly on the roof. As it continued I wondered whether it wouldn't be better to pitch nearer the deeps rather than setting up at the shallows, as I'd planned. The rain would be lowering the water temperature. I compromised, eventually, when the rain stopped, and set up my canvas behind the big ash at Bowskills. One rod was prepared then, after a final cup of tea at Barry's pitch (Pitchfords; John was in the Stile), I went back to the ash tree and dropped a hookful of corn under the overhanging branches. It was a cool night after the rain and I kept well wrapped in a blanket – leaping up at 3 a.m. as the line began to slide through the silver foil. The run stopped as I got my hands to the rod. I waited, then just readjusted the foil and didn't re-bait.

At 4 a.m. another rustling hiss shot me into the dawn and this time the line kept streaming out. I struck and a wave went away across the dim greyness of the water. Though the carp proved to be no more than eight pounds it led me a lunatic dance, diving under the branches and

A Record Carp Story

Redmire Pool, with Bowskill's tree on the left and the twin poplars of Pitchfords on the right.

tying the line into a complicated knot. I had to ask Barry to help get the little blighter out.

I made a cup of tea, thinking, as I sipped, that though it had been a muddle at least I'd grassed the first fish of the season.

The dawn was quite calm, after a restless night. John took Redmire's temperature: 67°. Shortly afterwards, he hooked and lost a big fish – using *macaroni*! Up in the shallows, I cast for a twenty-pounder that was cruising and bubbling just off the platform. The line tightened once, but it was too brief to hit. Creeping about after the obviously sullen and uninterested carp, I began to feel rather tired. Also, a serious-looking storm cloud was looming up from the west, so I had no qualms about crawling under the canvas for a few hours' welcome sleep. As I dozed off, the rain was sooshing down.

A big wind got up and disturbed my dreams. It rushed tempestuously into the ash tree above me, rousing me, making me think about heavy branches. Rain fell in torrents, but I was warm and dry and I just drifted away from it all. Then a tremendous clap of thunder shook me wide awake and I looked out to see the mid-day sky as dark as night. It cleared, even as I watched, and as the thunder cloud sank into the east the brightness above made it look even darker. Blue-black over Ross.

The wind was still powerful. Redmire was whipped into a rippling sea of waves. The water slapped against the roots of the tree and sparkled in the flashes of sunlight. I thought of another day like this one, though maybe not so turbulent, when I'd landed the forty-pounder. The weather couldn't have been more extreme, but huge fish are often stirred by such storms. This is what I was thinking, but I didn't do any fishing. As yet there were no carp visible in the shallows, but rather than move my bits down to the deeper water I'd wait and see what the wind pushed up to me.

I made a meal in the pump-house and then Barry and John came round and joined me. We sat and talked for an hour about the monsters we'd seen. We remembered the Bishop* and the King.

The sun was shining strongly and the wind had decreased to a strong, steady breeze. At about 8.30 p.m. we went back to our pitches and I saw that another grim-looking cloud was filling the sky.

I would fish the shallows until dark and rather than use the Mk IV, I now prepared the Walker-built Avon, proposing to couple it with the Aerial and eight-pound line. But when I tested the line I knew it was a daft idea – there was only twenty-five yards on the reel! So I got out the old Ambidex, with its new nine-pound line, tied on a gold size 8 (Mustad) and, using a float, cast in beneath the first group of willows. After twenty minutes with nothing but gudgeon flipping on the surface, I moved up to the '35' tree and cast again.

A light fall of rain began to whisper down, but it soon stopped, although the sky remained threatening. I re-cast and the float caught against a branch and flew off the line. I didn't bother to put it back. There was quite a powerful wind drift and I was having problems keeping the bait stationary. It would be wiser to fish free-line.

I could see some movement at the top of the shallows. Big fish were

---

*In the syndicate's parlance the Bishop was known as *'the old 38'* and the King was simply *'the enormous common carp'*.

stirring the water, making rose-shaped clouds of red mud. I crept up to Quinlans and thought I could see five carp feeding in the murk. One was a five-pounder, three were twenty-pounders and the other was like a sunken rowing boat. But they all kept disappearing into the mud clouds and it was difficult to know where to cast.

I'd baited with three grains of corn, and after squeezing a bean-sized knob of plasticine onto the line, cast out twenty yards to the right. A biggish fish swam in from the island, coming straight for the bait. He hesitated over it, but then cruised off. Then a twenty-pound common began to mill about below the floating algae, only two rod-lengths out. I dropped a bait in front of him and after a minute the line shot tight – only to fall instantly slack again. I cast twice more to the edge of the scummy algae, resting the rod in a twig and sitting back on an old willow stump. However, even though the breeze had died to a whisper, there was still a fair amount of drift, the floating scum caught the line, dragging the bait and so I reeled in and made another cast right in front of the large dark shape that was just then ghosting round the willow on my left. I almost botched it. Casting at that fish was like casting at the sun – I suddenly lost my focus in a fever of anticipation. But it was all right. The bait flew in a perfect arc and the fish must have taken it before it hit bottom.

I put in the pick-up and was just lowering the rod when I saw the line slithering across the surface. I couldn't miss and found myself connected to a fish that swirled round, making a colossal splash, and surged diagonally across the shallows. I let him run, having planned a neat dodge for such a circumstance. As the line brushed against the willow, I jumped in and floundered round to my right, ducking under an alder bough that was actually hanging into the water. I whipped the rod round the branch with the line still streaming off the spool, and waded on until I was standing at the mouth of the feeder stream. Now I wouldn't have to play the fish from the wrong side of a willow tree.

A huge tail had shown above the surface as the carp charged away, so I was fairly sure I'd hooked the rowing boat. Now, as I increased pressure, he answered me with a tremendous burst of power, making a tail-swipe that flattened out all the ripples in an area ten yards square. The explosive splash was heard (I later discovered) right at the other end of the pool. He was almost under the willows on the far bank, but with the line chiming near its breaking point, I swung him clear.

I began to whistle loudly for help, but there was no answer. The rats must be asleep, I thought.

The carp changed direction and made the move I'd feared most, heading back across the shallows towards the big willow branch in the '35' pitch. I saw a bow wave bulge suddenly upwards as he accelerated towards it. I piled on the pressure and the sidestrain swung him round towards me, so that he was now pointing at an even more dangerous snag – that submerged willow where we'd first made contact. I felt the bend going out of the rod as he came steadily towards me. There was no alternative but to suddenly cram on pressure again, hoping he would think I *wanted* him under the tree. He stopped dead and then, with another tumultuous splash, turned in his tracks and headed back down the pool.

I let him go, but he didn't retreat far enough and I had to ease off to a barely taut line. But he insisted on hanging dangerously close to the willow, so I picked up some water-logged branches and threw them at him. He wasn't impressed and wouldn't shift until I let the line fall absolutely slack, then he moved back along the margins until he was nearing the willow, forty yards away, and I had to tighten up and hold him hard. He stubbornly refused, though, to come out into the open water.

I began to shout and eventually John answered me.

"Bring a net!" I yelled.

"Where are you?"

"Up at the top of the shallows."

John came crashing and thumping along the overgrown west bank, rounded the top of the pool, splashed across the feeder stream and appeared through the trees behind me, puffing, bedraggled and dripping with muddy water. He waded out next to me, but realised the water was too shallow to net a big fish and so squelched onwards through the silt for another few yards.

Suddenly, I felt the carp heading out into the pool again and saw a wave cleaving through the grey ripples. Without a sound or a word Barry had come up under the willows and actually climbed into the half-submerged tree, causing the fish to take flight.

I steered the carp towards us and Barry had a good view of it as it ploughed past him. He said it was the Bishop, but I though he was joking and laughed – nervously.

"It's a big fish," said John, as a wave approached him.

A Record Carp Story

A great black back rose higher and higher in the water; then everything stopped. The fish had grounded itself just ten feet from the net.

I tried to drag it a little nearer, but it wallowed round until it was broadside on and I couldn't budge it. John, sinking waist deep into the silt, inched forward and began to slide the net under the fish. I had visions of the mesh catching the line and winced, saying, "Careful, I don't want him to thrash about now!" He pushed the net until its frame had enclosed the bulk of the carp, then he began to lift. For a moment nothing happened – he stuck, straining, and the mesh wasn't rising up.

"Lift! Lift it!" shouted Barry from the willow.

John heaved and there was a sudden eruption of mud and water. The bend went abruptly out of the rod and I thought for a moment that the fish had gone, but it was there, hammocked in the folds of the big net, with a load of mud, scum and weed.*

"Bite the line, John," I said, turning for the shore.

"You must be joking," he said, "I can't move!"

Splodging through the ooze and taking his arm I helped him to heave and wrest himself free. Then we began stumbling back to the bank, half falling, staggering under the weight that was in the net.

Barry came hurrying across the marshy field and helped us carry our load through the edge of the trees. He looked at the carp as we lowered it into the wet grass. It was difficult to see it *was* a carp – it looked like a black pig that had been rolling in the mud. He estimated the weight. "Fifty-three pounds." There was no emotion in his voice at all.

I can't remember what I was saying, nor what I was thinking. I'd known, as soon as John lifted, that we'd got a monster, a new record, but I can't recall exactly what was in my mind.

I carefully unhooked it, which was tricky as the hold was firmly in the leather-like bottom lip, then I ran for the spring balance and a pan

---

*This was easily the most impressive piece of netting I've ever seen. In his impossible position, John knew that he only had one opportunity to net what was obviously a record fish. One chance was all he needed.

Britain's biggest carp:
fifty-one-and-a-half pounds, caught on an old cane rod and an ancient Ambidex reel.

of water to wash the silty flanks. We cleaned off the mud and the carp was revealed in all its glory. My heart gave another lift as I realised that it was not only gigantic, it was also a beautiful specimen. Sleek and bright. Richly coloured – purple, ochre, chestnut, amber. It was tremendously broad and deep, but it wasn't gross ($36\frac{1}{2} \times 34\frac{1}{2}$ inches).

Gently, we slid the carp into a capacious sling and hoisted it onto the balance. The pointer on the dial swung round and stopped, quiveringly, at $51\frac{3}{4}$ lbs. Deducting the weight of the sling left 51 lbs 6 oz. I gazed at the dial for a few moments, then sat back in the grass blinking. After all these years, all those lost fish, *all these diaries*, my line finally led to this great dark-coloured mirror-carp – a fish I'd caught seven years before, when it looked too old and weary to grow bigger – but it had grown; it had become a different fish altogether and was now the monster that I'd called the Bishop. We lay it reverently on the grass and stared at it.

The sky was almost dark, yet over in the west, under the edge of the cloud, a strip of blue showed clear and cool looking, and in its centre, a thin crescent moon. The breeze had long ceased, the evening was perfectly still.

There were a few moments' awed silence as we crouched round the carp. Then Barry broke the spell.

"Yatesy's cracked it!" he laughed.

I stood up and threw my hat across the field.

PART VI

The Last Cast

After more than quarter of a century I've suddenly realised that I'm not fishing for a fish that is a biological parcel of bones, tissues, blood, fluids, muscles, nerves and flesh : I'm fishing for an image.
I have seen this image many times but, however flawless, it lacks that magical quality I keep hoping for. It links me with the landscape, but it never equals the strange beauty of the first carp I ever saw.
I sometimes curse that old man who fished by the willow, in the village pond, thirty years ago.

C.Y. Notebook (1985)

28

EARTHING THE CURRENT

A MIST is sliding through the woods. Looking from my open window in the half-light of dawn it could be the blurring of my sleep-heavy eyes, but the mist curls up, revealing the clear outline of an oak tree. Then, as the air leans in through the window, cold and clean, it breathes life into my senses. The midsummer morning smells like rain on roses.

Deep under the cottage a clock strikes four. From over the horizon, only audible when the air shifts from that direction, a skylark's song rises and falls. There are no other sounds. I creep downstairs, careful not to wake my sleeping wife, and quietly make a cup of tea and eat a simple breakfast. For a few minutes I sit and think how foolish I am not to get up more regularly before sunrise. Not only is the fishing excellent then, the world itself is a more interesting place; everything seems more intense, however shadowy the dawn, however subdued the uninhabited landscape. Even my cottage has an unfamiliar atmosphere; the objects in the rooms seem subtly changed, as if something had happened to them in the night. A vase of flowers, a pile of books, a cup and saucer, a bundle of rods; all appear to have some new identity. It is 4.15 a.m. and the rooms and the woods outside the windows are poised in that colourless, cloudy transition between dark and light.

Rod, net and creel are secured to the cross-bar and rack of my bicycle. Within a few moments the dawn's silence is blasted by a long roar that only I can hear – the rush of air in my ears as I roll fast and smoothly down the first steep hill. The lane flattens out and the roar subsides to a whispering flutter. I pedal easily along, past the still sleeping farms, past dozing horses and cattle, past cottages with billowing gardens and a modern bungalow with a garden like a graveyard, through the last pockets of vapour that still lie, cold and clammy, in hollows and valleys. As the half-hour ride progresses so does the dawn chorus and long before I reach the water every bird is in full song. At a bend, I turn off the metalled road and on to a stony track that takes me bumping and juddering down towards a just visible lake. I can see it as a series of misty pools between a line of oaks and willows. Earlier, in the summer, before the fishing season began, the nightingales were singing here, one of the few places I know where they always seem to return. But it's too late in the year to hear them now; their songs are always finished by Midsummer. I lean my bike against a fence, shoulder my gear and trudge off across the wide, rolling field, leaving a clear trail of prints in the dewy grass. At the top of a low rise, where the field slopes directly into the reedy lake edge, I have to stop. A sullen red sun is appearing through the level layers of vapour. However clear the sky, no two sunrises are ever exactly the same. How many have I seen? A thousand? Probably, yet I will never become a hardened drinker of them; though I am accustomed to them, they will never become clichéd. Sunrises will always affect me like a large brandy on an empty stomach.

The image of a tree is strangely projected through the mist as the sun curves up behind it. Then a gold beam swings across from my right. For a moment I feel the inevitable charm working on me. But, suddenly, the whole expression of the morning changes. A huge, dark shape turns on the surface, close in, near enough to see a dull gleam flash from its side. It slides under with a slow, slurring splash. The ripples wheel and widen, shuffling the reeds, creasing the reflected light.

I'm sober again. A big carp has stolen the sunrise and the next moment I am crawling furtively behind the reeds, fumbling as I set up my rod, threading the line through the rings with trembling hands. Yes, yes, the sunrise was tremendous, but there will be another to equal it tomorrow. Not every day, though, does one of the grandfather carp show himself and only very rarely have I seen one this close to the bank. Perhaps he was sniffing for the corn I scattered round here last evening.

In a surprisingly short time everything is prepared and I am creeping between the yellow-flowering reeds, wading to a yard from the edge of them. Then a long wait while I scan the water for further signs of fishy presence. There! A patch of bubbles, just a short distance from where the carp leapt; the sun picks them out like brass studs on the surface.

As well as the bubbles, there is a light vorticing, just a vague crinkle of water; the fish's tail is doing that; he is nose-down, browsing over the muddy shallows with his tail working gently just a foot or so below the surface. I overcast deliberately and before the hookful of corn has sunk I draw it back so that it quietly settles next to the feeding fish. He must take it. Will he take it?

The sun is high enough now to soothe away the last chill from the dawn and disperse the mist. The lake appears more open and expansive. I can see the far bank clearly and islands and swans. As I wait – the fish is ignoring me – I begin to notice the wider world again; what had become suddenly transformed and dramatic merges back into the placid, familiar beauty of this Sussex lake. Yet I know I'm not quite composed. There is what seems to be a faint buzzing in my ears, like the hum of a generator, and when I look back at the slack line, lying in the green surface film, it's too easy to imagine it drawing tight.

My heart trips and I blink as I see the actual movement of my line superimposed over my imagining. It twitches and begins to slide away, leaving a thin, dark trail in the layer of algae. The next second seems to break up lake and sky simultaneously as I sweep the rod up, the line slicing the water with a long fizzing slash. Everything solidifies. Then, slowly, a great shape comes bulging to the surface. In an eruption of spray, the fish whirls round and cleaves a bow wave towards a willow-hung island, thirty yards distant. The rod bends like a reed in a gale. I brake the reel with my hand and the friction scorches. In an effort to stop the run I pressure the tackle to its limits, and the line tings like metal against the rod-rings. At the last moment there

Earthing the Current

is a walloping splash and the carp swerves and turns, cutting round in a wide arc towards a half-submerged willow. I am convinced that tree is too far for him to reach, yet his power is tremendous and I am almost proved wrong.

As the fish is swung round once more I begin to feel calmer. The pull is still arm-wrenching but I know the battle is past the critical stage; I'm virtually in control now. The carp flounders and wallows, then lessens his resistance and allows himself to be drawn straight in, his broad, blue back breaking surface like the hull of an upturned yacht (the dorsal just like a keel). The net is ready and I'm amazed to realise that I'm standing almost up to my waist in open water, ten yards from my original position. I don't recall wading out. After a few last lunges and turns, the ripples flashing and the water spiralling in miniature whirlpools, I ease the fish gently over the mesh and heave it up. Staggering heavily, my boots clutched by the ooze, I slosh back to dry land and drag the net onto the grass.

Lying in the mesh is a glorious carp, like an exquisite, freshly varnished wood-carving. The large fins open like fans, the back glows blue, the sun reflects from each copper-coloured scale.

Whenever I get a good fish, that loose, vague connection I have with the landscape is immediately reinforced and clarified. Getting to grips with a part of the landscape, I suddenly feel accepted by it, more at home in it. It is, I realise, an ancient primeval link, but just because I live in the twentieth century does not mean I must live without it. If you are a live current you need to earth yourself now and then and there are not many better ways of doing that than by going fishing.

Just for a moment, I hold the splendid fish up. A perfect specimen, yet not really huge if I compare him to some of the monsters I've seen here. Irreverently, I weigh him and reduce him to a number on a scale which reads seventeen and a quarter pounds. His length is twenty-nine inches. Carefully, I carry him back to the water, wading out a few yards before I set him free. He balances himself on his broad fins and hangs a moment, recovering from his curious experience. The pectorals quiver, the tail sways, the gills puff and then, with unexpected acceleration, he arrows away into the lake, leaving a cloud of disturbed mud. Perhaps, in a few years, when he's grown older and heavier, we may meet again.

The Last Cast

The stillness has been nudged aside by the usual bustle of a summer day. A breeze is ruffling the lake, the clouds are beginning to form out of the blue sky, coots are squabbling and shrieking and someone on the far bank is leading the cows out from milking. My day is complete before it has properly begun and I won't cast again. I hadn't planned on getting back till lunch-time, but now I feel like another breakfast. And tomorrow, perhaps, I'll visit the river and try for a barbel.